Orphaned Warrior

By

Linda Warrior

CONTENTS

INTRODUCTION

I was born in Parkside Hospital, Middlesbrough, on 26 February, 1955 and lived with my mother until she encountered hard times.

On 3 December, 1957, through the various reasons I have written about, was placed, along with my elder sister, into one of George Muller's enormous old orphanages at Ashley Down, Bristol. There I resided until March 1958. After which time was moved to one of the Muller's smaller houses that became known as the 'Scattered Homes'. 'Severnleigh' was the name of the scattered home I was sent to. This house remained my home until the summer of 1966.

The amazing history of these orphanages dates back to the 1800s when they were founded by an incredible man, named George Muller.

Rebuilding my past began in 2002 while searching for a long lost junior school friend through a website named 'Friends Re-United'. I found the search for my historical truth to be a life-affirming, rewarding and poignant experience. The people working at Muller's Administration Office were kind enough to look through the archives to find the records of my personal history. These were very detailed; enclosed was all the correspondence between my mother and the Muller Homes, including some from the time before I was admitted in 1957. The letters revealed things about which I had no idea and gave me a very different perspective of the times and circumstances that had led to my admittance. They also gave substance to what had been, at times, an emotional experience for my mother and enabled me to see her as an individual - a real person who had faced her time without the social support mechanisms that exist today. If my mother hadn't been subjected to those hard times and been so desperate that she made the decision to place myself and my sister in the orphanage, I most probably would not have known about the good work these orphanages did - and still do to this day. For that, I am grateful.

George Muller homes in Bristol continue their good work today, actively working to help young people in day centres and provide retirement Homes for the elderly - not to mention the missionary work they do overseas.

All the correspondence that I have used in the writing of this book is copied word for word from the letters between my mother and the Muller home staff, which were kept and given to me personally by Muller's administration office in 2002. The rest of the book is an amalgamation of memories from various people who were involved in my life before and during the time I lived in Bristol at the George Muller Orphanage.

Even though there were moments I really did not want to be there and felt at times, that I desperately wanted my mother to come and take my sister and me home, where we could have a normal family life, I now realise how well-cared for we were, not only myself, but most of the children who lived within the 'George Muller Homes. I believe we were more privileged than some children during those times. I trust whoever may choose to read my story will appreciate this. I understand that not everyone has the good memories I have. Guess I was one of the fortunate children.

If the time ever came and it was necessary for me to be placed in a home for the elderly, I certainly would not object to being placed in one of the George Muller Homes.

Chapter 1

FIRST-BORN

It was the thirtieth of July, 1966, on a warm summer's day. The roads were a sea of cars bedecked with England flags. Lots of people were heading south to Wembley in London on their way to watch England versus West Germany in the 1966 football World Cup Final. The great Bobby Moore captained the English side, with Geoff Hurst scoring an equalising goal in the eighteenth minute and Martin Peters following with another goal in the second half. West Germany fought back to make the score 2-2 after ninety minutes, but Geoff Hurst secured the victory by scoring two more goals in extra time. 4 - 2 to England. I would never have thought that years later, during the year of 1995, while living in Malaysia and visiting Kota Kinabalu National Park, I would have the pleasure of spending the day with one of that game's greatest ever players, Bobby Charlton and his wife Norma. Soon after this, he was granted the title Sir Bobby Charlton by Queen Elizabeth II.

I wasn't really bothered about the World Cup, or anything else for that matter. Although I was aware of it through the other kids talking about it in the school play-ground and swapping their footy cards with each other that had the footballer's faces on them, these were given free with sweet cigarettes or bubble gum. I wasn't that interested in all of that hype going on in the playground; football hadn't been introduced into my life while living in the George Muller Homes for Children in Bristol. I had only one thing on my mind and it was far more important to me than any football game.

Filled to the brim with excitement I could hardly contain myself. The day had come that I had been waiting for, for a very long time! I was waiting patiently for my mother to arrive. She was coming to take me back home to Redcar, to live with her for the first time in nearly ten years.

One day, while I was looking through some old photos, I came across an old black and white one that my mother had given to me some years ago. Whilst studying it, I found myself reminiscing back to the days when it had been taken, although I was very young the memories managed to flood my mind. The photo had been taken in the garden of the grand old house named Severnleigh: This house was the second home in which I had lived in belonging to the George Muller homes. The picture is of my mother when she was in her early twenties with her two little girls - me and my sister Christine. We are sitting either side of her on the grass; flowers, bushes and a wall adorning the background. The picture had been taken in the garden of our new home during one of mother's visits 1958.

My mother was an attractive, well-presented lady, five feet four in height, with a slim, elegant figure. In the photo she is wearing a short sleeved black and white spotted dress, with white buttons and a white rounded collar attached. Her dress length is below the knee and flared out from the waist, probably with an organza petticoat attached, she is wearing white crisscross sandals to complement it. Her thick brown hair is fairly short, with a sharp parting and soft waves falling down just covering the left side of her low forehead and slightly shading her blue eyes. Her porcelain complexion allows her delicate mouth to stand out, enhancing her pretty smile.

My mother's first visit

In her early twenties, Phyllis Noreen Smith, or Noreen as she was known by her friends and family, who was the only girl out of four siblings, met a young man named Ted Warrior. They started courting and grew to love each other very much. After just a year of courtship decided they wanted to be married and start a family. On 18 August, 1951 Noreen married her chosen love in St John's Church, Middlesbrough Yorkshire. Talking to her about their wedding some years later, she told me that she and Ted had both been full of optimism and excitement about the life that lay ahead of them.

The newly-wedded couple started their married life renting a two-up, two-down terraced house, courtesy of a private owner, in Victoria Road, Middlesbrough. They weren't fortunate enough to have a garden, but were grateful to have a small brick and concrete back yard just big enough to hang up a washing-line. It contained a decrepit toilet without lighting and kept a torch handy so they could see to their way about outside in the dark. The toilet door didn't close properly and was literally just a few planks of wood nailed together and hung up with a few hinges. On flushing the chain, they were often splashed by the freezing water from the overflow. It was always a mad dash to get back into the warmth of the house on those dark and cold winter nights. The small living room was kept warm by the roaring fire that Ted made each day from pieces of coal, wood and paper plus the sea coal that had been collected from the beach and wrapped tightly into cone shapes from old newspapers.

The kitchen was even smaller and was so bitterly cold in the winter that leaf-veined ice designs embellished the windows and their breath nearly froze. They needed to wrap up just to go in there to make a cup of tea! Hung on a big hook on the back of the kitchen door was a large oval tin tub, which they used for strip washing in front of the fire. They didn't have central heating, but there was an immersion heater for hot water. It was very rarely used as it was so expensive, so they used boiling water from the kettle.

The bedrooms were always freezing cold during the winter months and a hot water bottle went to bed with them each night.

They didn't have an upstairs toilet, so a bucket was kept in the bedroom in case it was needed during the night time. Shaving and washing took place in the kitchen as it was slightly warmer downstairs when the fire was lit. In the summer, if the weather was nice, the windows and doors were opened so the house was warmed by the heat of the summer day - but there were occasions when the fire needed to be lit, even during the warm months.

By November, 1951, four months after they were married, Noreen became pregnant. Their happiness began to deteriorate as Ted had started going out to the pub a lot and was spending more and more time there, leaving her alone at home. He had begun drinking quite heavily, which led to her experiencing intermittent violence at his hands. She put up with this even though she was extremely scared, because she hoped it might stop after the baby's birth. July was approaching and as Noreen was getting nearer to her delivery date, Ted had calmed down and was being more attentive to her plus he had cut back on his drinking.

On 27 July, 1952, a beautiful baby girl was born - welcome to the world, Christine. She was an adorable baby with chubby cheeks and fine fair hair. Noreen and Ted were very happy with the birth of Christine. They had her baptized a few weeks after her birth in St. John's Church, where her Ted and Noreen had been married. My Nana Smith, who was my mother's mother, told me that in those days parents were encouraged to have their new born babies baptized within the first few weeks of being born in case there was any danger of early death.

Not that long after Christine's birth, the arguments between Noreen and Ted flared up again and the marital home was strained once more. Ted went back to drinking heavily and with that, came renewed violence, only this time it was worse. Noreen had hoped it would stop completely after her baby was born, but often Christine would witness her mother getting a beating from Ted. This violence had a knock-on effect on her and she became a nervous, over-sensitive child that would cower down when anyone raised their hand. This was not an ideal environment for the child or Noreen.

Noreen decided she'd had enough. She couldn't take anymore and told Ted they needed to separate. He agreed and went back to live with his mother, leaving Noreen and her daughter Christine get on with their lives as best they could. Noreen was finding it a struggle, as support from Ted was irregular and he kept coming back and forth whenever he felt like it, constantly making her life a misery.

During her separation from her husband, Noreen was invited to a friend's wedding. At the wedding she met some new people, one of whom was a man named Richard, known to his friends as Richie. He was a fair-haired, handsome, thickset but rugged sort of man. Richie spent most of his time travelling at sea, working in the Merchant Navy. There was an attraction between Noreen and the rugged, smartly-dressed man Richie and they began to see each other a little more often, although after all the abuse she had suffered, she was quite vulnerable. He showed kindness and affection to her, something she hadn't experienced for quite some time.

While out one evening with Richie and some friends, Noreen had had a fun night and quite a bit to drink that affected her more than she'd realised – the next morning she woke up in bed with Richie. She was very upset to say the least, because even though she had suffered abuse from her husband Ted was the man she really loved. A few weeks later, feeling a bit unwell, she visited her doctor and found out she was pregnant with Richie's baby. Noreen was still legally married to Ted and really didn't need another complication in her life as she was only just managing with Christine. On the other hand, Richie was really pleased and very attentive to her, but Noreen simply wasn't in love with him. This made things difficult as he wanted so much more than she would offer him. As Richie spent most of his time away at sea with the Merchant Navy, it meant Noreen spent nearly all of her pregnancy alone and caring for Christine on her own.

Noreen was woken up on a chilly Saturday morning in late February, 1955 with a few twinges here and .there. This didn't bother her unduly and she went about her day looking after

Christine. By six o'clock that evening her twinges had turned into stronger and more frequent pains, she realised she was now in labour. She walked with Christine to the house of her father, Walter Smith. Leaving Christine with him, she then set off on the trudge to Parkside Maternity Hospital, a fair distance from where she lived in Victoria road. The walk along with the constant labour pains wore her out. By the time she reached the hospital she was exhausted and was well into her labour, it didn't take too much longer before another baby girl had been born at nine o'clock, tipping the scales at 7 pounds.

Christine had a baby sister – me! My dad Richie was due home from sea at that time and was informed of my birth by a neighbour. He was overjoyed with the news and came straight up to the hospital to visit us both. Between them, my parents named me Linda.

A couple of weeks after my birth, my dad went back to sea and my mother was left alone, with two children to look after and care for and apparently not much support from either of the fathers. My mother arranged for my christening as soon as possible, for the same reasons Christine had been, I was also christened by the surname name of Warrior as she wanted both Christine and me to have the same surname. Just a few family and friends were at my christening, which was held at a different church to where Christine had been christened: St Michael's, Waterloo Rd, and Middlesbrough.

As it turned out, Christine and I were to become good companions for each other during the years that lay ahead.

When my dad, Richie, went back to sea, there wasn't any contact between my mother and him and it was appearing that he may have deserted her. He hadn't sent any money to her for my upkeep and she never knew where in the world he was. She was struggling with two of us on her own so she decided it might be best to go and see Ted, Christine's dad, to discuss whether it would be worth getting back together. After all, he was the man she still loved. I was now four months old and she hoped she would at least have a bit of a home life with Ted for herself and her two girls if she went back to him. After a discussion with Ted they agreed to try again and he moved back in with her, but it wasn't too long before he went back to his old ways: out drinking all the time and coming home drunk, which led to quarrelling, violence and beatings. He was breaking her heart and being nothing but a bully to her.

There was a time, (in my mother's words) during a very heated argument upstairs, he turned on me, picked me up and threatened to throw me out of the window, I would have been about five or six months old at the time as it wasn't long after he had moved back in with us. My mother was terrified for me and was screaming at him to stop and put me down. Finally he did, but he was still raging and stormed down the stairs where he started hitting Christine about her head. She was scared to death; crying and cowering away from him. Eventually he calmed down and went into a drunken sleep, leaving my mother and her girls traumatised. Another time, while trying to attack my mother during one of his drunken outbursts, he accidently knocked me into the fire guard that was placed in-front of the fire. As it fell down I went with it and landed into the fire, suffering very bad burns to my head. I needed to visit the hospital daily for the dressing to be changed. I still have the bald spot at the back of my head where my hair never grew back. My mother was heartbroken to see me in so much pain and often cried for it herself and because of what the man she loved had done to her and her children. He didn't care about my mother the way she cared about him and he certainly didn't care about us children, only his drinking. This bullying went on for months until the time came when my mother couldn't take anymore. She took into account the arguments and violence and whether or not she could carry on. She made a decision to leave Ted - for our sakes if not her own. They separated again and took Christine and me back to live with her father, Grandad Smith, in his small house. He was living alone as he and Nana had split up a few years before. There would be no going back to Ted this time. She applied for a divorce, which was granted on the grounds of mental abuse and cruelty. That was the end of the relationship.

My mother and Ted were finally divorced on 19 October 1956. By the time the divorce came through, Ted was living with another woman in Middlesbrough whom he had wanted to marry and had already had more children with her.

While the three of us were residing with Grandad Smith, our presence in his home took its toll and we were becoming an enormous strain on him. Even though we were at a nursery during the day-time, it became hard for him as in the evenings and at weekends, he would need to look after us while mother went to work. This was far from being an ideal set-up as he, being an elderly man, found it hard to tolerate two children of such a young age. There always seemed to be a problem of some sort and this extra strain on him was affecting his health.

There was a time, while we were living with Grandad Smith, my dad was onshore and my mother let him take me to see his mother and sisters for a few hours. The few hours turned into a lot of hours; the day had passed and my dad still hadn't any intention of bringing me back. By eleven o'clock that night, my mother was very worried. She went to the police to see if they could help to get me back. The police went round to my dad's house and informed him that he had no legal right to keep me. He told them he would take me back to my mother, but he had no intention of doing so - and he didn't.

My mother waited all the next day and on into the evening, by ten o'clock that night she went to the police again and got them to go with her to collect me. Reluctantly, my dad handed me back, but he wasn't happy. He had wanted to take me and Christine to live with him and his mother and sisters, where he said we would have been looked after well and my mother wouldn't have had to struggle on her own. (At least he cared enough to want to take us, more than Christine's dad) My dad turned against my mother and was angry with her for a long time after that, punishing her by not contributing to my upkeep. Christine's dad wasn't much better – he only paid something when he felt like it.

My mother tried to feed and clothe us the best that she could, but because of the lack of funds she found it to be a huge struggle to make ends meet. She did whatever work she could, cleaning toilets, scrubbing floors, serving petrol, factory work, barmaid - anything she could find and that meant having a day and an evening job just to earn a bit of money so she could provide for us. Unfortunately, she could never hang onto a job for more than a month. Grandad couldn't cope whenever one or both of us were ill, which meant she'd have to take time off to care for us and this would often end up with her losing her job. She was finding it more and more difficult - at one point she went through six jobs in three months.

In March, 1957, I developed Chickenpox followed with German measles. In April, Christine caught German measles then in June she caught chickenpox. Christine then developed a mild form of infant eczema and also had a tonsillectomy. By this time, my mother couldn't cope with it any longer. Christine was now aged four and I was one and half. My mother had had enough of begging at the Social Security, who had kept her waiting for hours on end for a measly five shillings. Five shillings may have been worth a bit back then, but it was not enough to keep the three of us for two weeks. Desperate and at her wits' end and not knowing which way to turn, the constant struggle of trying to feed and clothe us was breaking her heart.

With little or no money coming in from either of our fathers and with the pittance she received from Social Security not stretching far enough, my mother thought long and hard about what to do. She approached her father for advice, she told him that she was considering turning to prostitution as there wasn't any other way she could think of to provide for her girls. Obviously Grandad didn't want his daughter to be earning a living in this way. Instead, he suggested she should meet with a probation officer and discuss us girls being placed into a George Muller orphanage in Bristol until she could straighten herself out. Grandad had known of the officer through my Nana as she had placed my uncle, my mother's youngest brother, in one of Muller's Homes in previous years - but that's another story, as they say. The probation officer arranged a meeting with my mother and Grandad. The three of them held a long discussion about placing us girls into one of Bristol's George Muller Homes for a while until she was in a better financial position to care for us. The officer suggested that mother write to the Muller Home and ask for their help …

And so she did.

Chapter 2
GEORGE MULLER ORPHANAGES

Janet and Derek Fisher - Bygone Bristol Books

George Muller was born on 27 September 1805 in Kroppenstaedt, Germany. As a young boy, he cheated, was a liar and a thief, who would often do terrible things to his parents. In his teens, he landed himself in jail. Although he thought a lot about his bad behaviour of the last few years while he was there, it made no difference. On leaving prison, nothing had changed and Muller continued to rebel.

It began to look like George Muller was never going to reform. His future looked bleak until one day in the middle of November 1825, a man he knew named Beta, happened to mention the bible meetings that he had been attending. Muller was intrigued and wanted to know more. 'What happens at these meetings?' he asked Beta. 'We read the Bible, we sing and pray and then normally someone gives a sermon.' Beta replied. 'I'd like to go with you this evening' Muller said. 'I'm not so sure you will enjoy it' Beta replied doubtfully, but Muller had already made up his mind to go. Beta called for him that evening and off they went. Although he didn't realise it, this was the evening that would change his life forever. Only one month later, Muller became a Christian and began to study the Bible seriously. From that time onwards he wanted to become a preacher and teach God's word.

On 15 August, 1829, Mr. George Muller proposed to his love, Mary Groves and on 7 October, 1829, they were married with a simple service conducted by the Reverend John Abbot. Mary supported her husband in everything he did.

In 1829, they arrived in London, England where he trained as a missionary.

By 1830, he had become a pastor of a church in Teignmouth in Devon. In April 1832, George and Mary Muller moved to Bristol.

In July, 1832, cholera had broken out and by August, the outbreak had reached horrifying proportions. The funeral bell was ringing all day. During September the epidemic showed no signs of easing and in the middle of all this Mary was due to give birth. As her labour began, Mary became very ill; thankfully her illness was not cholera and she went on to give birth to a little girl named Lydia. Lydia was the Muller's only child to survive infancy.

By the beginning of October, 1832, the epidemic had reached its peak.

On 19 March, 1834, Mary gave birth to a son, whom she and Mr Muller named Elijah. Tragically he was only to survive fifteen months before pneumonia claimed his young life.

During 1834, George Muller and a friend of his, a Scotsman named Henry Craik, who had been converted to Christianity while in University, founded the *Scriptural Knowledge Institution (SKI) for Home and Abroad.* In the seven months following its establishment, the institution had provided Sunday school education for over a hundred children, day school education to over two hundred children and adult schools for around forty adults. SKI's good work also included provision of a thousand Bibles and New Testaments along with fifty seven pounds that was sent to missionaries abroad.

By 1835, Muller had been thinking a lot about the orphans in Bristol, which had now become one of Britain's major social problems. Children were living in filth in the streets, destitute and nowhere to go since they had been orphaned due to the typhoid and cholera epidemic.

In earlier years, while a student at Halle in 1826, Mr Muller had lodged for two months in one of the great orphan houses built in the seventeenth century by Francke, a professor at the University of Leipzig. Mr Muller never forgot the experience and thought about offering similar care to the ever increasing orphans of Bristol.

On 21 November, 1835, Mr Muller stated that 'today I have had it very much impressed on my heart no longer merely to think about the establishment of an orphan house, but actually to set about it'.

Mr Muller prayed. 'Dear God, will you please provide the premises, one thousand pounds and suitable staff to look after the children'. Mr Muller had learnt to rely on God alone for the needs of his own family and now he was looking to him to house, feed and clothe an altogether larger and needier family. He prayed to God for every single penny he received to build and run the homes. One day after praying to God, he received the first shilling for this orphan house. Later that day, he received another shilling from a German man and in the afternoon, he was generously given his first piece of furniture and a large wardrobe. Another kind person from Ireland sent him ten pounds for his institution. The Lord had given him in a short time about fifty pounds, when he had only asked him for forty. Mr Muller had made a life-long decision never to ask anybody for the things he may have needed, but to rely on prayer to God alone. In the first year, he had received just over one hundred and fifty pounds; in the second year nearly two hundred pounds and in the third year, the enormous sum of two hundred and sixty-seven pounds, fifteen shillings and eight pence.
This was a great financial encouragement for him. It is known that Mr Muller's accounts never lacked precision and he

was convinced more than ever that he was doing the right thing, and that his belief in God would guide him.

Mr Muller addressed a meeting at which he outlined his proposals for the children's home. He said the home would only be established if God provided the means and suitable staff to run it. Under no circumstances would any individual be asked for money or materials. There would be no charge for entry into the homes, or restriction on the grounds of class or creed. All who wished to be taken on as assistants, matrons or masters would have to be true believers in Christ and qualified for the work ahead of them.

As the weeks went by, Mr Muller accumulated clothing, furniture, crockery; in fact, everything he would need for the home. He paid rent for a year on a large terraced house. 6 Wilson Street. Thirty children were housed in that home. By April 1836, he had two orphan houses in Wilson Street, between them housing sixty girls.

In June, 1837, Mr Muller decided to open a third home. This was to be for boys aged seven and above. By the end of 1837, eighty-one children and nine full.-.time staff were sitting down to meals in the three homes. There had been enough applications to fill another home with girls aged seven and above, plus more applications for infants than the homes were able to accommodate. Three hundred and fifty children were taught in the day schools run by the SKI and three hundred and twenty children attended the Sunday school.

During October, 1845, a few years after establishing the small homes, Mr Muller received what he described as a 'polite and friendly' letter from a resident of Wilson Street. The letter read that the resident and his neighbours were in various ways being inconvenienced by the orphan houses in Wilson Street and by the noise they created during play times. Mr Muller had to decide what action to take. As usual, he prayed to God for guidance about his new problem. He then decided the solution was to build a house large enough to house all the orphans. However, he was going to need around ten thousand pounds and also a large plot of land to do so. He discussed this at length with his wife, Mary.

Mary Muller's sister returned from a visit to London, where she told Muller she had met a Christian architect who was very interested in Mr Muller's work. The architect had offered to draw up plans for the large orphanage building and supervise construction, free of charge.

On 10 December, 1845, Mr Muller received his first donation towards the new building and then set about looking for six or seven acres of land somewhere on the outskirts of Bristol. While continuing saving for the orphan house that he wished to have built, Mr. Muller heard about a piece of land going cheap on Ashley Down. After viewing the land and thinking it would be suitable for his needs, he decided to buy it. The following evening he came to an agreement with the owner of the land. From then on his dream became a reality. The architect had finished drawing up the plans by the end of April, 1846.

It was fifteen months later in July, 1847, before any work actually started on the new building due to the British economy suffering a crisis and with many railway companies being called into question, leading to financial panic. The winter of 1846 – 1847, saw a catastrophic crop failure of wheat and potatoes. The American cotton crop was also well below expectation, sending prices soaring. In May 1847, Mr Muller recorded: 'Never were provisions nearly so expensive since the beginning of the work, as they are now. The bread is almost twice as much as it was eighteen months ago, the oatmeal nearly three times as much, the rice more than double the usual price and no potatoes can be used, on account of their exceedingly high price'.

By June, 1847, the economy had improved and money was coming in again, he estimated the building project would cost no less than fourteen thousand, five hundred pounds. Some things he wanted with the building were not required initially and could be built at a later date, like the three play-grounds and a small road. He therefore decided to go ahead and start the work on the orphan house No1. The first workmen arrived on Ashley

Down in July, 1847. The foundation stone was laid on 19 August, and all the while, Mr Muller continued to receive money towards his new home. He also received one hundred pounds for a new suit of clothes for every boy in Wilson Street; another requirement for which he had been praying to God for.

Throughout the winter when the weather was as its best, the work proceeded on the new building. By the following May it was already at roof level. Mr Muller spent long hours making final preparations before he could receive the first children into the new home, praying that the total cost would be met. Over eleven thousand pounds had been given, but he still needed three thousand pounds more in order to complete the work and fittings. Soon after this, fifteen hundred pounds was donated; then, on 11 February, 1849, Mr Muller received an anonymous visitor. This visitor had been following Mr Muller's work and filled him with great inspiration. The anonymous man had intended to leave his money to Muller's Homes in his will. He then had a change of heart and decided instead to donate the money in his lifetime when it would be of more use, the visitor handed Mr Muller two thousand pounds - cash.

Conrad Finzel, one of Bristol's Aldermen, was a religious man *'The Good Conrad Finzel'* as he was affectionately known as, was a benevolent man. He was the owner of a sugar refinery which was destroyed one day in a massive fire. He had it rebuilt on an even larger scale. Mr Fiinzel was a wealthy man, and was reputed to have given at least ten thousand pounds a year to Muller's Orphanage at Ashley Down. It's said that he eventually became the major donor to the Bristol orphanages.

On Monday 18 June, 1849 - with great excitement at Wilson Street: the first children were ready to move up to Ashley Down, House No. 1.

Although Mr Muller now cared for three hundred children, he still had a long and growing list of children seeking admission. By December 1850, seventy-eight more names had been added to the list and by 1856, had grown to nearly eight hundred and fifty names. Mr Muller found it distressing to turn any one of the children away and began to think about building another home. This one would need to be large enough to accommodate seven hundred children, which would make a grand total of one thousand children that Mr. Muller had provided with a home.

In January 1851, Mr. Muller received a large donation for his work: three thousand pounds. He used the money to start saving for his next home while keeping the existing one going. All this was achieved through prayer and human kindness.

By November 1857, Muller's House No.2 had opened, next door to House No.1, on Ashley Down. Mr Muller immediately started thinking yet another home was needed for the thousands of children requiring care, this one had to be large enough to house four hundred and fifty children. By September 1858, he had chosen the land, opposite houses one and two. A benevolent glass manufacturer had offered to supply the glass for the three hundred and fifty windows, free of charge.

Even while house No.3 was being built, he was thinking about yet another home and decided he would build not one, but two more homes on Ashley-Down for eight hundred and fifty children. Eventually he would care for over two thousand children. On 2 March, 1862 the largest of the buildings opened, Ashley-Down house No. 3.

Many of the children, including teenagers, had been unable to read when they first arrived at the homes. On 11 April, 1836, a young girl by the name of Charlotte Hill was to be the very first child received into the care of Mr Muller's orphanages. Mr Muller described the joy of educating hundreds of children, who otherwise would have had no intellectual development and teaching them a variety of life skills, so that they could become useful members of society. He added that all the mental and physical improvement he provided for the children would never have been satisfying had he not been able to benefit them spiritually too. This blessing had been able to do concerning not twenty or fifty orphans, but hundreds.

By the end of May, 1862 and money still coming in, Mr Muller announced his intention of enlarging his work to cater for two thousand more children. On 5 November, 1868, Guy Fawkes' Day, the fourth home was opened and on 6 January, 1870, Mr Muller opened his fifth and final orphan home.

Over twenty years had elapsed since Mr Muller first announced his plans to build his orphan homes. By this time Mary Muller was seventy-two years of age and for a year or more it had been apparent to Mr Muller that her health was deteriorating. She was getting progressively thinner and tiring very quickly. Mr Muller tried, unsuccessfully to persuade her to work less and eat more. Two years earlier, she'd mentioned to her husband she thought she was getting too old to carry on, but believed the Lord would allow her to see houses four and five furnished and opened. Indeed the Lord did allow her to see both houses opened and throughout 1869, she spent nearly every day at work in the buildings.

Mary Muller passed away in 1870 after No 5 house had been finished, leaving Mr Muller and their only daughter, Lydia. Nearly two years after Mary's death, Lydia persuaded Mr Muller to re - marry. He had known Miss Susannah Grace Sangar, a governess from Clifton, for more than twenty-five years as a consistent Christian and regarded that she would prove a great helper in his various services. They were married on 30 November 1871, and for the next two years, Susannah learned everything about her husband's work and gave him as much help and support as she could.

In March 1874, Susannah developed a fever and typhoid and by early April she had become delirious; the fever was at its peak and the worst was feared. However, Susannah recovered from the typhoid and went on to lead a full life, travelling to numerous countries with her husband, helping him with his work

Mr Muller's daughter Lydia married Mr James Wright on 16 November 1871 in Bethesda Church, Bristol, where Mr Muller had obtained the position of Pastor. Her devoted husband, James, in later years became Mr Muller's successor in the running of the orphanages.

During the month of January 1890, while Mr Muller was on a tour in India preaching, a letter was put into his hand from a missionary from Agra, to whom Mr Wright had sent a telegram, informing his father-in-law of his daughter Lydia's, untimely death. The sudden bereavement forced Mr Muller to bring his mission tour to a close and depart for Bristol so he could mourn his daughter and comfort Mr Wright. Lydia was fifty-eight years of age and had been a capable and cheerful supervisor of many important domestic arrangements where a woman's hand was needed. She had kept watch over the wants of the orphans as her dear mother had done before her. Lydia's death greatly affected her husband, James and especially Mr Muller, who had had such a strong bond with his beloved daughter.

Aged seventy-three, after twenty-three years married to Mr Muller and being by his side, Susannah died on 13 January, 1894. A year after Susannah's death Mr. Muller launched worldwide preaching tours until old age began to make him weary. Even then, Mr Muller was heard to say, 'It's 1898 and I am feeling quite young in comparison to friends ten years my junior. I am in my ninety-third year without rheumatism, aches or pains and I can still do my ordinary work at the orphan houses with as much comfort to myself as seventy years ago.'

On 9 March, 1898, Mr Muller was sitting at his desk at No.3 house, working as usual when he turned to Mr James Wright and said, 'When I got up this morning I felt weak and had to rest three times as I dressed. 'Do you think you should have an attendant in your bedroom to help you dress?' asked Mr Wright.
'After tomorrow,' replied Mr Muller. Later in the day he told Mr Wright that he felt fine and quite himself again. In the evening, Mr Muller led the usual weekly prayer meeting in No.3 house, and concluded by announcing the hymn, '*We'll Sing of the Shepherd That Died*'. Mr Muller joined in with the last verse:

'We'll sing of such subjects alone

None other our tongues shall employ

But better His love will be known

In yonder bright regions of joy'

Mr. Muller said goodnight to James Wright that evening and climbed the stairs to his bedroom. Recently he had been waking up feeling hungry during the night so a staff member had been kind enough to leave a glass of milk and a biscuit on his dressing table should he be in need of it. He had a peaceful night and in the morning he woke between five and six o'clock. He arose from his bed and slowly walked to his dressing table, on doing so he suddenly fell to the floor, it was then he was touched with a moment of glorious reality and Mr Muller was greeted by his Lord and saviour.

Mr George Muller passed away at the age of ninety-two on 10 March, 1898. His funeral was held on the 14 March, 1898. It is written that nothing like it has ever been seen in Bristol before or since. Thousands of people lined the route of the procession; flags were flown at half-mast; black shutters were put up; and people drew their window blinds. Nearly one hundred carriages, including the mayor's state coach, joined the procession across the river to Arnos Vale Cemetery where a crowd of several thousand people had gathered at the main gates. Stewards cleared an opening for the bearers to carry Mr Muller's coffin up the hillside to the spot under the yew tree where Mary and Susannah had been buried. The service at the graveside concluded with the enormous congregation joining together to sing the very same hymn Mr Muller had chosen at his final prayer meeting less than five days earlier; ending, not in sadness but, as Mr Muller would have wished, in 'Yonder bright regions of joy'.

The city of Bristol mourned.

Mr Mullers Funeral

Mr George Muller

Feeling proud and honoured by George Muller's Grave in 2010

George Muller's Grave. Both his first wife Mary and his second wife Susannah are buried along with him in Arnos Vale Cemetery, Bath Road, Bristol.

The inscription reads on Mr Muller's headstone

IN LOVING MEMORY OF
GEORGE MULLER,
FOUNDER OF THE ASHLEY DOWN ORPHANAGE
BORN SEPTEMBER 27TH 1805
FELL ASLEEP MARCH 10TH 1898
HE TRUSTED IN GOD WITH WHOM NOTHING SHALL BE
IMPOSSIBLE, AND IN HIS BELOVED SON JESUS CHRIST OUR
LORD, WHO SAID GO UNTO MY FATHER AND WHATSOEVER
YE SHALL ASK IN MY NAME THAT WILL I DO. THAT THE
FATHER MAY BE GLORIFIED IN THE SON, AND IN HIS
INSPIRED WORD WHICH DECLARES THAT ALL THINGS ARE
POSSIBLE TO HIM THAT BELEIVETH AND GOD FULFILLED
THESE DECLARATIONS IN THE EXPERIENCE OF HIS
SERVANT BY ENABLING HIM TO PROVIDE AND CARE FOR
ABOUT TEN THOUSAND ORPHANS
--------------------0--------------------
THIS MEMORIAL WAS ERECTED BY THE SPONTANEOUS
AND LOVING GIFTS OF MANY OF THESE ORPHANS

Photos on display in the museum

George Muller's amazing memorabilia is kept in the museum at Muller House, 7 Cotham Park, Bristol, and can be seen during office hours. George Muller's work continued to flourish to this day in day-care centres and homes for the elderly.

Chapter 3

ONLY FOR A WHILE

On 28 September, 1957, my mother wrote to the George Muller Homes, pleading for their help.

Dear Sir
I am writing to you in full hope that you can help me?
I prayed to God last night and he gave me my answer this morning in the form of your annual report 118th which I read regularly, you send it to my brother as he was in one of your homes up until 1954.
The whole point is I am divorced from my husband and I have two little girls aged four and nearly two. I cannot seem to keep a job more than three to four weeks. I am up to my eyes in unpaid debts, the children see very little of me and have been in a day nursery practically since they were born and on the whole I'm thoroughly at my wits end.
I would like you to know that my husband did not father my youngest child and this is reflecting on us all in a lot of ways and making us all very unhappy.
I should like to work solidly to pay off all my debts and save for a home of our own, without someone to take care of my children, I can't.
Believe me I've tried so very hard and now I am writing to you to see if you can help me by taking care of my children.
I know this is God's way of answering my prayers. He knows how much I have cried for his help.
I will leave the matter rest with you. I feel sure in my heart that you will do all you can.
God bless you
Mrs P N Warrior.

Muller's Homes received the letter and the following people were approached regarding my mother's request:

- Mrs Cooper, the probation officer in Middlesbrough.
- Mr B Brown at the NSPCC, Middlesbrough.
- Mrs Horne, the welfare officer in Bristol.

- The matron from Parkside Day Nursery, Middlesbrough.

The response to my mother's letter from the Muller's Homes:

Dear Mrs Warrior
We are very sorry to hear of the troubles you are in and will most certainly consider whether we can help by receiving your two little girls here.
Forms will be sent to be completed also you application will need to be supported by a responsible person, who knows of your circumstances, i.e.: health visitor, a welfare officer or a minister of your church.
Were you given custody of your girls at the time of your divorce and was the divorce made on the grounds of your unfaithfulness or the grounds of cruelty by Mr Warrior?
This is entirely confidential but in taking your children it is a great help to know as much as possible about their circumstances.
We remember your brother being here of course and hope he is getting on well.
Yours sincerely
Mrs Horne.

On 4 October 1957 my mother wrote to Muller's

Dear Mrs Horne,
Thank you for your letter dated 30th September.
Your words have helped me a lot and it's nice to know someone cares about our welfare.

The original letter my mother wrote asking for Muller's help

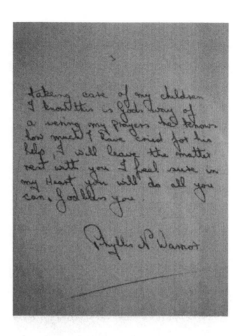

I was granted a divorce on the grounds of cruelty by Mr Warrior. He is now wishing to marry the girl whom he is living with and is also bearing his child.

Linda's father is away at sea but has an address in Middlesbrough. He does not support her and I will do so myself. Mrs Horne, I do not want you to think I have no thought for my children. I love them dearly, I have only the wish to do right for them and am convinced we will never be happy or have a normal life if we go on the way we are at the present,

At the moment they see little enough of me. I have just found out that my babysitter is unreliable and she has left the children on their own with no one to attend them if they wake up!

I had a part time job as a barmaid in a club. I have lost that job today due to Linda being poorly with the flu.

Christine is a sensitive child due to the life she shared with her father. She was there so often when he hit me, now she is afraid to death when anyone raises a hand. She is on the whole a good child who reacts normally to love and understanding. She is also very advanced and has a good head for school.

*The children have been in Parkside Day Nursery for quite some
time, in fact the Matron knows them better than I do.
I shall let the matter rest in your care for the moment and hope to
hear from you soon.
God Bless. And once again, thank you.
Sincerely yours
Mrs Warrior*

Enclosed with the letter, was a copy of Christine's birth
certificate.

On 8 October 1957, Muller's staff wrote to the probation
officer in Middlesbrough regarding my mother's application for us
to go into the homes.

*Dear Mrs Cooper,
Mrs Warrior of Victoria Rd Middlesbrough has given your name as
supporting her application that we should receive her two little girls
into our care.
We should be as grateful for your observations in this case as we
should be very willing to receive the children if they really need a
home, which their mother cannot provide.
We would be very sorry to encourage her to part with them and
break up the family unless it is really necessary.
It seems such a long way to send these children from their
mother; it will also be difficult and expensive for her to visit.
On the other hand, it is sometimes better to take the children from
an undesirable environment and we should certainly make it
possible for the mother to see them when she was able.
We should be very glad to have your advice on this case before
making any final decision.
You probably know that Mrs Warrior's brother was in the care of
these homes until he left school and that is the reason for applying
to us.
Yours Sincerely
Muller's Homes*

Mrs Cooper, the probation officer, replied to Muller's on 11
October, 1957

Dear Mrs Horne,
Thank you for your letter from 8ᵗʰ October.
Mrs Warrior called to see me earlier this week to discuss her application to have the little girls placed in your care. She has had a somewhat difficult and unhappy life in the past few years and I understand she has already told you about her divorce and parentage of Linda.
There is an order in existence against her ex-husband that he should pay her three pounds and five shillings a week, she very rarely receives this and in any case finds it impossible to adequately keep the three of them on this amount.
It has therefore, been necessary for her to go out to work, but if there is anything wrong with the girls she must take time off. They have been ill recently and she has not worked for about a month and has not received any money during this time.
Because of this, the girl now feels that it would be far better if the children were placed in a home, and of course, the reason for choosing your home is the fact that her brother was there. However, another reason is that the father of Linda has caused trouble on previous occasions when he has returned from sea. On one occasion he took Linda away and was missing for several days and, quite naturally, this is most upsetting for the child let alone the mother.
Mrs Warrior is fully aware that she may have some difficulty visiting the children when they are so far away. I am sure she has not come to her decision lightly, I am also in the opinion that should you decide to accept them into your home it will be in the children's own interests.
Mrs Cooper (probation officer)

More and more people were being involved, all wanting and needing to find out about my mother's background. A letter from Muller's welfare officer to the National Society for the Prevention of Cruelty to Children in Middlesbrough was written on the 8 October, 1957, asking if they had come across the case at all.

Mr Brown replied on behalf of the NSPCC:

*I am sorry I have no personal knowledge of this family, except I
have seen and heard the elder of the children, Christine I believe?
And her language is shocking!
The mother is well known in my district, her house is only hundred
yards from my own.
She is always dressed in the height of fashion and the children are
well clothed.
I believe she works in a club in the evenings.
The youngest child is illegitimate and the father is at sea.
I have heard she is contemplating marriage, but I am sure that is
just idle gossip.
My wife, while shopping in the district has also heard gossip of
another nature, which I will not repeat.
Yours faithfully
Mr Brown.*

Personally my feelings, for someone who stated in the
beginning of his letter that he had no personal knowledge of my
mother, certainly had a lot to say about her.

I don't think Muller's were too impressed with Mr Brown's
reply and a 'thank you' note was forwarded to him. Muller's
continued to check out the history of the care we had received
with my mother.

Another letter was sent to the matron at the day nursery
we had attended in Middlesbrough. The Welfare in Bristol asked
to know a bit more about us children and if there were any
difficulties for which they might have to be prepared. These
included whether we were developing mentally in a normal fashion
and if we had received proper physical care at home.

The matron's reply of 18 October, 1957

*Dear Madam,
Both children have attended the nursery since babyhood and have
gone through the usual phases of difficulties attached to growing
up.
You ask for any particular difficulties.*

Christine did have a trying period at the age of four. I felt this was due to misunderstanding at home. The child was continually being told by various people she was not a nice girl like her sister Linda, therefore lived up to this reputation. At the nursery her behaviour was quite normal and was a perfectly happy child.
Christine has started school now and has been back to us many times since. She seems quite well and happy.
An Eczema condition which lasted about three months which occurred when Christine was three years old cleared after treatment at the skin clinic and has not occurred since.
Infectious diseases: whooping cough, German measles, chicken pox and dysentery.
Linda is a sweet little girl, but can be very obstinate; she can be persuaded but not compelled.
Infectious diseases: German measles, chicken pox and dysentery. Both children have developed mentally quite normally.
Christine has always shown great preference to domestic play of all kinds and loved to be in the home corner playing with dolls and cots, giving her a younger child to mother was the height of happiness for her.
These children could have received better physical care at home. The mother has been under difficulties living with an aged father who has not been very sympathetic towards the children.
Regards
Matron
Middlesbrough Day Care Centre

A letter was sent to the matron from Muller's, thanking her for her careful and considered account which would be most helpful if and when the children were received.

Chapter 4

THE DECISION

On 15 October, 1957, my mother received this letter from Mrs Horne, the welfare officer at Muller's:

Dear Mrs Warrior,
Your application for your two children to come here has been considered, we shall be glad to receive them as soon as possible. We are at present having an epidemic of influenza and should like to be sure of getting through that before any new children come to us.
It may be two or three weeks before we can take them. I will let you know definitely about this later, I hope that with this prospect In view it will make it possible to manage until they come.
I enclose a medical form for each for you to take with the children to your family doctor to be completed, also a form of agreement for you to sign yourself.
The shortened form of birth certificate for Linda will be sufficient for you to send, it will not be necessary to send school reports as they are so young.
You will be able to continue drawing family allowance for Linda provided it is paid over to us. I am not clear whether the one pound court order and two shilling dependent's allowance comes per week or per month. If it is a weekly allowance then the amount due to be paid would be 22/- for Christine and 8/- family allowance for Linda each week.
This can be collected and sent to us every four weeks if that is more convenient. I hope you will be able to bring the children before so that we may get to know each other and straighten out a few points then.
Yours truly
Mrs Horne (Muller's welfare officer)

On 15 October, 1957, this letter was written by Mrs Horne, the Muller's Welfare Officer, to Mrs Cooper, the Probation Officer in Middlesbrough.

Dear Mrs Cooper

Thank you for the information you gave about the children and their mother.
It seems as though we could help by taking them as soon as possible.
I hope very much that Mrs Warrior will continue interest and responsibility and not drift away onto anything undesirable, feeling that she is freed from any responsibility for her children.
I will write to her as soon as we receive them and shall be glad to know that you will be keeping in touch with her after they come.
We shall be very glad to let you know at any time on our side how things are going.
Mrs Horne.

In the meantime, my mother applied to the WRAC (Women's Royal Air Corp) for work. Hopefully she would get a job with them and start paying off her debts would be able to get us back to live with her as soon as possible. She had her interview with the WRAC - and now it was their turn to start writing letters to Muller's Welfare Officer.

Dear Madam,
The above named woman has applied to join the WRAC
On the interview today she said she had been negotiating with you about the care of her two children. I understand you are prepared to accept the girls into your home. If this is so, I would be most obliged if you would confirm this as I have to be satisfied that the children are to be cared for before I can go ahead with Mrs Warrior's application.
Yours faithfully
Captain G (WRAC)

The reply from Muller's to the WRAC, 18 October, 1957.
Dear Sir,
In reply to your enquiry we have agreed to receive Mrs Warrior's children into our care. This has been done on the advice of the probation and local N.S.P.CC Inspector. It will be at least three to four weeks before we can receive them.
Yours Sincerely
Mrs Horne.

On 26 October, my mother wrote to Mrs .Horne sending the completed forms, the health cards and my birth certificate. She wasn't able to send her marriage certificate as it still hadn't been returned from the solicitors. My mother was broke and she asked the probation officer Mrs Cooper, if there was any way she could get some assistance with travelling expenses to Bristol. My mother promised to pay the money back when she had the means, but if she couldn't borrow it then she would manage somehow. Mrs Cooper replied that mother should ask Mrs Horne.

Unfortunately, my mother was refused the help she required and had to find another way. She was hoping that Muller's would soon be clear of the flu epidemic they were suffering so she could get us girls settled in there. The problems continued at her father's home and was worrying about my dad causing trouble again as his ship was due in. Every time he came home, he managed to find a way of upsetting her and us girls and could be really nasty. He had never forgiven my mother for preventing Christine and me from living with him and his family.

On 30 October, 1957, Mrs. Horne wrote to my mother:

The forms have arrived to us safely and I think that's all we need for the children. I will let you know as soon as possible when we can receive them.
With regard to travelling expenses we do not advance money for this and it would be better if you could arrange from your own people, or possibly the local N.S.P.C.C. would help you, though I am not sure of this as it is not their case.
I am interested to hear that you have applied to join the W.R.A.C; perhaps it may be wise to get right away from your present surroundings for a time at any rate.
You say you are doing this, however to make something of your life, but it is not the place where you are or the work you are doing which will make a difference to your life.
If you would give yourself to God, trusting in Jesus Christ as your saviour to set you free from all the old bad things, that is the best new start you can make and would be a strength outside yourself

to hold on to where ever you go. I do hope you do this and find what a difference it makes to your life.
Mrs Horne

The Forms:

26th October 1957
THE MULLER HOMES FOR CHILDREN
Ashley Down, Bristol 7
Children for whom application is made – CHRISTINE & LINDA WARRIOR
Relatives or friends who undertake to make arrangements for the children if it should become necessary for them to be removed from the homes.
To be signed in each case by the person named:
Name: Phyllis N Warrior
Address: 127 Victoria Road
Relationship to child: Mother
Occupation: Barmaid
Signature
Agreement: to be signed by parent or guardian responsible for the children.
I have carefully considered the conditions of reception and wish to place Christine and Linda Warrior in the care of The Muller Homes for Children. If accepted I will keep to those conditions and undertake not to remove the children without the consent of the directors.
Signed: mothers signature
Relationship to children: Mother
Address: As above
Dated 23 / 10/ 1957

3. AGREEMENT – to be signed by the parent or guardian
   responsible for the children

I have carefully considered the conditions of reception and wish

to place _Christine & Linda Warren_

in the care of The Muller Homes for Children. If accepted I will
keep to these conditions and undertake not to remove the children
without the consent of the Directors.

Signed _Phyllis M. Warren_

Relationship to children _Mother_

Address _124 Victoria Rd_

Middlesbrough

Date _23-10-57_

To be sent with this form –

1. Medical Form completed and signed by a qualified doctor

2. Birth Certificate for each child – _Christine's received_

3. Marriage Certificate of parents

4. Certificates of Death of either parent

*The form my mother needed to sign for Christine and me to go
into the orphanage*

THE MULLER HOMES for CHILDREN
Ashley Down, Bristol 7

Children for whom
application is CHRISTINE & LINDA WARRIOR
being made

Relatives or friends who undertake to make arrangements for the
children if it should become necessary for them to be removed from
the Home
To be signed in each case by the person named:

Name *Phyllis N. Warrior*   Occupation
Address *124 Victoria Road*   *Barmaid*
Relationship to child *Mother*
Signature *Phyllis N. Warrior*

Name   Occupation
Address
Relationship to child
Signature

Name   Occupation
Address
Relationship to child
Signature

The form arrived on 13 November, 1957. It was finalised; Christine and me were going to live in a Muller's Orphanage. All that was needed was the date of our arrival.

A letter arrived in the post for my mother from Muller's.

Dear Mrs Warrior,
We could receive your two little girls on Tuesday 3rd, Wednesday 4th or Thursday 5th of December 1957, and I should be glad if you would let me know as soon as possible which day you can travel.
If you can stay overnight in Bristol I suggest that you write beforehand to the C.A.W.G Hostel in Wellington Park, Blackboy

Hill Bristol 8. Accommodation there is very nice and not at all expensive.
There is no need to worry about the children's clothes as we will be expecting to provide what they need, but you could bring anything that is in good order. See that they bring a favourite toy so they have something familiar, but I'm sure they will settle down very happily.
Yours Sincerely
Mrs Horne (Muller's)

Now my mother had a date for us to go into the homes, or near enough, now she could start to plan what she was going to do.

A letter from my mother to Mrs. Horne dated 15 November, 1958.

Dear Mrs Horne,
Just a line to let you know I did receive your last letter. I just want to tell you what I'm going to do.
You are right, it is not the place or the people who matter and I do with all my heart put my trust in God and give myself to him as he is my saviour.
Thank you for your kind and helpful words.
I have made up my mind not to join the W.R.A.C
The pay is not enough to pay off my debts let alone save. I want to save for my own home, it will take quite a few years to get enough but I pray with the help of God I shall succeed.
I have got expenses from my father, I have a home and a job to go to in Liverpool, my girlfriend and her husband have kindly asked me to share their home and a friend has found me a job with her in Littlewoods Pools Office.
Her manager wants to know how long it will be before I can start, so now I leave it up to you. I hope to hear from you soon.
The children are both well.
I have been explaining to Christine she is going away and is quite looking forward to it. I think it's the prospect of a new school.

*Linda will take no settling in, she can settle down anywhere and
she does.
God bless you.
Mrs Warrior*

My mother was having second thoughts about joining the
forces at this stage. Meanwhile the WRAC was writing to Mrs
Horne:

*I thank you for your letter Mrs Horne, I am wondering if you have
the children with you yet? If they have arrived could you let me
know to enable me to proceed with Mrs Warrior's application to
join the W.R.A.C?
I assume that the home will take complete responsibility of the
children and I would be most grateful if you could mention this in
your reply.
Yours Faithfully
Captain*

Mrs Horne wrote to Captain in the WRAC on 18 November,
1957
*Dear Madam,
With reference to your enquiry about Mrs Warrior's children we
expect to receive them here on Dec 3rd and I confirm that we shall
take responsibility for them.
I should perhaps add that in Mrs Warrior's latest letter to me, she
said she had given up the idea of joining the W.R.A.C & hope to
take a post in Liverpool. I do not know what she really will do, but I
thought this information would be of interest to you.
Yours Faithfully
Mrs Horne*

Mrs Horne also wrote to my mother on 18 November, 1957
*Dear Mrs Warrior,
I write to confirm that it will be quite alright for us to receive the
children on Tuesday December 3rd, we expect you here about 4
o'clock. Will you be sure to bring the milk token book for Linda
Yours Sincerely
Mrs Horne.*

Chapter 5

HEART-BREAKING

3 December, 1957.

Up bright and early. We children had a busy day ahead of us but it would be an even busier and more exhausting one for my mother. Our best clothes were all packed and my much loved toy fluffy rabbit was squeezed tightly in my arms, while Christine was hanging on to her favourite toy whatever that might have been.

We had a long train journey to make from Middlesbrough to Bristol, Temple Meads train station; a journey that was to take up the whole day. For Christine and me it was an adventure, but for my mother it was to be the saddest day of her life. Once she'd left us in Bristol, she would have had no idea how long it would be before she would be able to see us again.

By four o'clock in the afternoon we arrived at the monstrous house which was to be mine and Christine's home for the un-for-see-able future: Ashley-Down House No.3. I was too young to remember my first memories of the house, but I returned in later years to look around the huge, old looking building that had been built with pennant stone, dressed with plain freestone. It had long and empty corridors with what seemed like and hundreds of never-ending rooms. It looked very much like a hospital and was informed that it has been used as part of the setting for the televised hospital drama *Casualty*.

It felt surreal knowing I had lived in the same building that had housed thousands and thousands of orphans since the 1800s.

Following our arrival at Ashley-Down House No.3, Christine we were taken to a large reception room where we waited for a member of staff to come and settle us in.

The Reception Room

Janet and Derek Fisher - 'Bygone Bristol' Books

Mean-while my mother completed the formalities needed to leave us there. After a while it was time for her to go. Reluctant to leave and hugging us both tightly in her arms, she then had to say her goodbyes to both Christine and me before heading out on her long, lonely journey back to Middlesbrough without us.

It broke her heart to leave us behind that day.
On 6 December, 1957, my mother wrote to Mrs Horne.

Dear Mrs Horne,
I left Bristol on the 7.20pm train and arrived back home at 5.30am.
I do hope the children are not fretting? I shall write a letter to
Christine tomorrow, so perhaps you will let her keep it?
I can't find my marriage lines but will send them as soon as
possible.
Trusting you will let me know how the children are. Goodnight and
God bless you all.
Sincerely
Mrs Warrior

This is the reply from Mrs Horne to my mother:

Dear Mrs Warrior,

*Thank you very much for your letter to hand enclosing the milk
token book for Linda.
I am sure you will be glad to know that the girls have settled quite
happily with the other children so do please set your mind at rest
about them.
I'm sorry you had such a trying journey, but of course the distance
is so great. I hope that things will straighten out now that you have
settled your little family.
Please send your marriage certificate when you come across it, if
you are unable to trace it perhaps you could get a copy please for
our files.
Yours Sincerely
Mrs Horne*

Eighteen days had passed by since my mother had left us at Muller's and there were only a few days left to Christmas. I had only ever spent one Christmas with my mother as I wasn't two years of age yet. Christine and I weren't going to be together with my mother this year as we would be spending Christmas in the orphanage. It was going to be a very sad Christmas for her without us.

My mother wrote to Mrs Horne.

Dear Mrs Horne,

*How are the children getting on? Christine I hope is not fretting. I
shall send a parcel this weekend, and I trust you will know best
what is right for them.
I should like you to share whatever chocolate and sweets there is
amongst the other children, as my neighbours are all sending
some, they think of Linda and Christine very much.
I have found a place of work and will start next week.
There has been no money placed in the Town Hall from
Christine's father, so as soon as I get to work I shall send
something out of my money.
I have summoned my ex - husband so perhaps that may bring
results, I shall let you know.
I am just trying to get over not having the children but it will be a
long time before I get used to it. I should like to see them, do you*

think it will be alright at the end of February, Linda's birthday, they should have settled really well by then, I shall take your advice of course, so please do let me know.
My brother says he will come and visit them sometime, he is still in the Navy and stationed in Plymouth.
Well Mrs Horne I will take this opportunity to wish you a very happy Xmas and may God is with you always.
Please tell me if my letters to Christine are not right as I don't always know what to say and I don't want to put down anything that I shouldn't.
Goodnight and God bless you always.
Mrs P N Warrior

Mrs. Horne wrote back, pleased that my mother had found suitable work near home so she wouldn't have to leave her own people. Mrs Horne said we had settled in well and Christine was going to school with other girls her own age, she was enjoying it very much and Mrs Horne thought she would do well there. Mrs Horne also told my mother she could come and visit at the end of February on a Saturday; but not on my second birthday, as mother had suggested, as it was a Wednesday.

Mrs Horne wrote:

You will understand that we cannot take the children out of school to see visitors or we would be doing this the whole time for everyone.
Perhaps you would be able to come down on the Friday evening and stay somewhere in Bristol so as to have most of Saturday with them.
Christine will love to have your letter, and it is a great help to us when parents are as co-operative as you are.
With all good wishes for Christmas and the New Year
Mrs Horne.

My mother was not aware of it at the time, but she had already lost us to the Muller's home. I think she was under the illusion she could take us back fairly soon. From then onwards, she would have to ask permission to see her children. The orphanage didn't take kindly to making allowances despite knowing how far she had to travel. Rules were rules. The first Saturday in every month my mother was allowed to visit. If she missed that date because of work or whatever the reason, she would have to wait until the next visit was due. There were exceptions on occasions such as school holidays, but these exceptions were very few and far between.

Our early days at Muller's

On the Downs

Good companions - at Severnleigh

Me – Three years old at Severnleigh

Chapter 6

GETTING AWAY

On 4 January, 1958, my mother wrote:

Dear Mrs Horne,
I just want to let you know I have come down to London to work. I
had to get away from home for a while.
Christmas made me realise how much the children meant to me.
My friends who were in Middlesbrough for Xmas with their little girl
asked me down here, so perhaps I will be happier here and It's
not quite so far to see the children.
I am just settling in this week and will get a job for next week.
I have written to my solicitor asking him to sort out my case as Mr
Warrior is up before the magistrate on the 10th January for arrears
on my maintenance order, until then I can't say what money I can
send.
It is worrying me as you have had the children for one month now
and had nothing for their keep.
How are they?
Still happy I pray, and did their parcel arrive alright?
Please write soon, I love to hear from you, I know you are busy
but your letters mean so much to me.
New address: Romford Rd, Manor Park, London
God Bless you always
Mrs Warrior
PS. A very Happy New Year to all

This is the reply from Mrs Horne dated 7 January, 1958

Dear Mrs Warrior,
Thank you for letting me know your new address.
I hope you will be successful in finding work that suits you and will
settle down happily.
The children had a lovely time at Christmas and have had other
parties since. Christine does like your letters, and I am so glad you
write them regularly. I think that if you come to see them when you
can afford to do so they are settled enough not to be upset.

We can understand how much you miss having them with you, they are dear little girls and very good companions, I am sure that the hope of making a home for them again keeps you busy trying to get your affairs straightened out as quickly as possible.
With all good wishes for 1958
Yours Sincerely
Mrs Horne

My mother's reply of 15 January, 1958:

Dear Mrs Horne,
Thank you for your letter and good wishes. I have found a nice little job and I have got good lodgings with friendly people. I have the chance of a lift to Bristol next Sunday morning from a young couple who live in the same place as me. They would also bring me back, so I wondered if you would mind if I came to see the children on Sunday. I am working each Saturday and can't manage to get off work, so PLEASE Mrs Horne would you let me know as soon as possible whether this would be suitable. I would so much like to see the children and this seems a very good opportunity. I shall await your reply as my friends would like to know fairly soon just what I'm doing.
I have not heard yet from the court what is happening but they have promised to let me know quickly. I think that's all for the moment so cheerio and God bless you.
Mrs Warrior

Mrs Horne wrote back to my mother:

Dear Mrs Warrior,
I am so sorry to disappoint you, but we do not have Sunday visiting, if we made an exception in one case would very soon have to allow a whole lot more and the homely Sunday we make for the children would be spoiled.
You will find that any considerate employer will allow you to take a working day off now and then if you explain about your children not being with you, or I can write officially to ask for this if you prefer it.

During the school holidays, when Christine is at home in the week,
you can arrange to come on another day if Saturday is really
difficult, and of course then you get the advantage of cheap day
trips quite often.
The children are back at school now, having enjoyed some
wonderful parties during the holidays. Christine and Linda are both
keeping well and Christine is not nearly so shy now, she even
makes friends with some of the boys and the men staff that she
wouldn't even look at to begin with.
I am so glad you have lodgings with friendly people and also like
your work.
Yours Sincerely
Mrs Horne.

My mother was devastated. She couldn't take time off work and never seemed to be able to visit her girls when she was free through various reasons. It was she who was fretting, not us. She wrote a letter on 26 January 1958, asking if it would be possible to see her children on another Saturday.

Dear Mrs Horne,
Would you be kind enough to grant me permission to see the
children this coming Saturday at approximately 4pm?
I do hope they are keeping well and behaving themselves.
I attended the court with Mr Warrior on Friday the 24th January
1958 and the magistrate will inform Mr M (not sure who he is?)
that I have signed the various papers giving full permission for the
maintenance of Christine to be paid directly over to you.
Trusting the reply I receive will not be disappointing.
I remain yours faithfully.
PS. Would you please give Christine the enclosed letter?

Christine really loved receiving letters from our mother and as she improved with her reading skills, loved reading them out-loud to me.

On 28 January, 1958, Mrs Horne wrote:
Dear Mrs Warrior,

Thank you for your letter this morning, I am glad to know the court business has gone through satisfactorily. It will be a relief to you to have all this settled.
We shall be pleased for you to see the children on Saturday, I have given Christine your letter and they will be looking forward to your visit. As you will only have a short time here, we will arrange for you to have some tea with them upstairs so as not to waste any precious time you might have together.
Yours Sincerely
Mrs Horne

Finally, my mother was going to see her girls, even if it was only for a couple of hours. She was also granted a visit at the end of February, which she made sure she attended even though she wasn't feeling too well.

On 4 March, Mrs Horne from Muller's wrote to my mother.

Dear Mrs Warrior,
I have looked up the records and find that the money from Middlesbrough Court has begun to come through, so that matter evidently is quite in order.
Thank you for making the arrangement for this.
I do hope you are feeling better now than you were on Saturday, and that the journey did you no harm. It means such a lot to the children to know that you will come regularly to visit them, and the reason they part from you so happily and without a fuss is because they trust you to come again next time, and this helps us too in caring for them when they know that both you and we are doing the best we can for them.
Yours Sincerely
Mrs Horne

A day out in Bristol

On Holiday in Minehead

Chapter 7

'THE SCATTERED HOMES'

As the years went by the cholera and typhoid epidemics ceased, there was a large reduction in the number of orphans coming to stay in the Muller homes. In addition, many of the elder boys and girls had grown up and left so there was no longer the need for houses as large as those on Ashley Down. In 1958, the large houses became the Bristol College of Science and Technology, the property of the local Education Authority. Smaller family group homes were bought in Bristol, Clevedon, Weston-Super-Mare and Minehead to house the remaining girls and boys. These new houses soon came to be referred to as the 'Scattered Homes'.

Moving from Ashley Down to the 'Scattered Home's in March 1958

Janet and Derek Fisher - 'Bygone Bristol 'Books

Muller orphan homes vans

Janet & Derek Fisher – 'Bygone Bristol' Books

Christine had been going to Sefton Park Infants School in Ashley Down. Muller's wrote to them to say Christine would not be returning after the end of the week as she was being moved to one of the scattered homes in Stoke Bishop. Christine and I were going to live in a new house named *Severnleigh*: a lovely big house at the top of the Downs. There were going to be fourteen children living there, plus the 'aunties' and the animals.

On 14 March, 1958, Muller's wrote to my mother.

Dear Mrs Warrior,
We now have room for Christine and Linda together in one of our small homes and are moving them at the end of this week. They will still be in Bristol and just as easy for you to visit. The address is:-
'SEVERNLEIGH'
1, STOKE HILL,
STOKE BISHOP
BRISTOL 9.
The housemother in charge there is Miss Hilda Ashton. She has a mixed group of children all of various ages and is particularly experienced in caring for small children as she used to work in our nursery here.
Visiting day is still the same, and I hope you will be able to go up there next visiting day and get to know the staff. A number two or a twenty two bus both stop at the top of Stoke Hill quite near the

house. You can get number twenty two outside Temple Meads
Station on the other side of the road, or a Number two from the
centre.
Yours Sincerely
Mrs Horne

Christine and I were moved to Severnleigh on the 26 March, 1958. Our new family included Shawn, the family dog; I made friends with him immediately as I loved dogs, he was a beautiful black and white pointer who would excitedly come bounding over to greet me with a sloppy wet lick, ears flapping up and down, often knocking me over. We also had Fiona the tortoise who would disappear for days on end, then re-appear out of the blue from time to time, usually when it was time to put her into a box to hibernate for the winter. Auntie Hilda had our gardener paint her name on her shell with white paint to make her easier to find in the garden as she was forever wandering off and getting lost. We had two cats: a Siamese named Sophie and a tabby that we named Tabby. Every one of us was brought up to be kind to and love all animals.

There was our gardener, Mr Brooks, who came in every day. I still remember that man with great fondness. He was a tall, robust, thick-set, solid man with the kindest face and the warmest smile I've ever seen. He would wear a flat cap, which he always respectfully removed on entering the house and hung it on a hook in the kitchen near to the oven, he usually wore a navy blue or brown bib and brace type overalls, but occasionally would wear tweed trousers that were held up with a belt or braces. He always wore a collarless shirt with the sleeves rolled up. I really liked Mr Brooks. Maybe he was the daddy I didn't have? Nevertheless, he was my favourite person and Shawn was my favourite animal in Severnleigh.

Auntie Hilda, who was our housemother, was in charge of the daily running of the home. She was quite a stocky lady with short greying, curly hair, who had an oval shaped-face with a large double chin and rosy cheeks. She had a stern face and a faint, but hearty laugh and had an even warmer smile. Auntie Hilda made the rules and disciplined us so much in her matronly way that we were all terrified whenever she was on the warpath about something. We all knew when to stay out of her way as she could be a bit of an ogre and quite frightening with it! On the other hand, she had a gentle and funny side to her that we all saw many times. She wore either pink or blue glasses and would clean them with the hankie that she kept stuffed up her sleeve - regardless of whether she wore a long or a short sleeved top. Most importantly of all, she cared for each and every one of us as we were her family and she was our mother.

Auntie Grace originated from Cardiff in Wales and was put in charge of the house whenever Auntie Hilda had to go away on business or the like. She was very warm-hearted and rarely got cross with us, a plump and fairly plain lady, but as I remember she would often wear a nice brooch on the neckline of her jumper. I can also remember the car she owned, a green Volkswagen Beetle and sometimes took Christine and me or any of the other kids with her to visit her mother in Cardiff for a weekend. I think she liked the company when she was driving.

Auntie June was a beautiful, elegant lady, inside and out, always softly-spoken, bubbly and vibrant. I remember her being the kindest auntie out of them all and nothing was too much trouble for her to help us. Her blonde shoulder-length hair always looked immaculate with its flicked out curls. Auntie June would cut our finger nails and she showed us how to care for them by pushing the cuticles back. She had lovely nails and I wanted mine to be like hers and I would often mould plasticine round my finger nails and over the tips to look like I had long nails! She was always impeccable and every one of us loved and admired her. Chris and I had the greatest honour of being her bridesmaids when she and Uncle John were married in 1963.

Auntie Margaret, I think, may have been the youngest of the aunties. She was the up-to-the-minute trendy auntie who loved her music, mini-skirts and modern sixties' hair style. She always wore open toed sandals in the house and we all knew when she was around by the sound of her sandals flip-flopping on the linoleum lined flooring around the house. I liked her style, and wanted to be like her when I grew up.

Auntie Ruth was a bit old fashioned, but lovely with it. I can't say much about Auntie Dawn as I don't remember her too well, other than the fact she was a gentle lady. Auntie Heidi was our German auntie, who would try and teach us German while doing the washing-up after meals. All I remember is how to count to ten in German, so she didn't really succeed with me.

The Children of Severnleigh

Linda Warrior

Christine Warrior

Ruth

Paul

Arthur

Jackie

Sandra

Mary

Christine

Jean

George

Hazel

Keith

Margaret-She didn't live with us permanently, only during holidays from boarding school. For various reasons I cannot use the surnames of the children named above, however, these people who were my surrogate brothers and sisters, will always hold a special place in my heart.

Severnleigh House

SEVERNLEIGH

This magnificent building stands proud in its own grounds, adorned by hundreds of well-established trees and shrubs, surrounded by an old grey wall and wrought-iron gates. Built with hefty out-of-shape stone bricks in different colours, and with a beautiful, feature stained glass window on the first floor round to the left, Severnleigh is unique and grand. It stands adjacent to a memorial cross on a small hill just off the Downs and has a tarmac driveway leading to the stunning entrance; stone steps up to a substantial bright red front door with round beige stone pillars either side.

At the bottom of the garden, there was an oval shaped pond the size of a small swimming pool with a gate and mesh fencing around it for safety. It was filled with all different-sized fish, some of them grew really big and we would be fascinated watching their babies following them around the pond. In the winter months if the weather was cold enough the pond would freeze over. We would look for the fish and see them motionless below the ice looking like they had died. Miraculously, they came back to life when the ice melted in the spring! There was frogs spawn that we collected and nurtured until it developed into tadpoles and then frogs. We had newts, water lilies, rushes and everything that you would expect in a garden water feature. It was a magical place surrounded by fir, pine, conker and acorn trees. When the conkers fell from the trees we collected them, fed string through them and played a game of conkers with each other, smashing each other's conkers to bits. Whoever had any left was the winner.

To the left of the pond stood a slide and a double swing, on which we would compete to see who could go the highest. The boys were always better than the girls.

There was one shed at the bottom of the garden big enough to house all the tools and lawnmower, there was another that held tricycles, scooters, balls, skipping ropes, stilts, dolls prams and go karts made for us children by our gardener Mr Brooks. There was something for each and every one of us to enjoy when we were able to play outside during the nice weather. To the left of the garden path was a substantial vegetable patch, providing all the seasonal home-grown vegetables needed to feed us. Sometimes Mr Brooks would give us seeds to plant so we could have a little garden project of our own to tend to.

On the right hand side of the garden, behind the tall trees, were large hills covered with grass and flower beds. These were Auntie Hilda's pride and joy and were usually out of bounds to us. The only exception was in the winter when the snow was on the ground and we would be allowed to take out old unused kitchen tin trays and sledge down the hills. It was great fun for all of us children and even the younger aunties would join in with snowball fights. During the winter, after a good snowfall and it laid thick on the ground, we would roll virtually all of it up and make the biggest snowman we could, using a carrot for a nose and coal for the eyes, gloves for hands and one of Mr Brook's old caps plonked on its head. We'd place our snowman in front of the dining room window so we could admire it at meal times while watching it slowly melt over time. Usually we weren't allowed in the wooded areas where the compost heap was kept, as this was Mr Brook's domain. Also, the odd grass snake had been known to appear, so best we stayed away.

To the left of Severnleigh's front door was the kitchen. Its walls were painted magnolia and its high windows virtually touched the ceiling, giving it a bright and airy feel. On the back wall was an oversized cooker, with heavy doors and plenty of cooking rings. Hanging on the wall near the oven where Mr Brooks kept his cap, was a poppy made from wax that I had bought for him a couple of year's previously with a bit of money I had saved. I knew something was wrong one morning when Mr Brooks hadn't arrived on time as he was never late. He hadn't been feeling well of late, that morning Auntie Hilda gathered us all together, then gently told us children that he had gone to heaven. She then handed me the poppy and said Mr Brooks would have wanted me to keep it. Shawn pined for him dreadfully. I will never forget Mr Brooks. It broke my heart when he died and left a massive hole in my life that day, but, I still have my precious memories of this wonderful man whom we all loved and cared for.

Against the right wall of the kitchen, stood the largest well-stocked, double-door, white fridge with great silver handles, it was always stacked with enough food to feed an army. To the right of the draining board, was the cutlery drawer and just below that was the dreaded wooden spoon drawer! Besides being used for stirring in cooking, these wooden spoons were used to wallop our hands as punishment if we had been naughty. When these occasions arose, which they did all too often, we would be sent to fetch the dreaded 'wooden spoon'. Each time we'd come back with a small one, but we never got away with that and we'd be sent back to get the large one.

'Hold out your hand and take your punishment' auntie would say, as we jumped up and down trying to back away hoping they would miss, 'Sorry Auntie, sorry Auntie.' Ouch that would hurt. Occasionally they got their aim wrong and missed, walloping themselves with the wooden spoon, it gave us sheer delight for us to watch, while their face turned to a glowing shade of red with embarrassment just before she had dished out our pain! It never did me any harm though.

As we grew older, at approximately eight to ten years of age and depending on how sensible the child was, we were given a job to do in the kitchen to assist with making breakfast each morning. My job was to make the toast. I was never that good at it and quite often burnt it, why the aunties let me keep on doing it, I will never know. They must have had faith in me and I got there in the end and without setting the kitchen on fire too! My sister Christine's job was to make the porridge and one morning she caught her arm on the handle of a pan, knocking boiling milk over herself. We could hear her scream of pain all around the house. The emergency doctor was called out to the house to treat burns on her left arm and leg; thankfully she wasn't scarred for life. However, after that she wasn't to be trusted with a pan of milk again. Instead she was charged with peeling two pans of spuds for the aunties' lunch, along with filling the coal scuttles ready for Mr Brooks to stoke the ovens.

Auntie Hilda kept a small transistor radio on the kitchen window sill – I always wished for one of my own, ever since I heard music I guess, but had to wait for a few years before I got one. Auntie Hilda never had it on for music, but sometimes on a weekend there would be a programme she wanted to listen to; usually the Archers or Jimmy Clitheroe. I loved it when she had to go out and left Auntie Margaret in charge of us as she loved music and would have it on in the playroom while doing the ironing!

After each meal, the aunties and children all shared the chores of washing, drying and putting away the pots. The aunties took it in turns on different days to do the washing-up as we younger ones weren't capable, while Ruth, Jackie and me walked around the kitchen on our toes, pretending to be ballet dancers while drying up the dishes. We all had our little dreams for the future.

Between the kitchen and the playroom was a large hall table which always displayed a vase of seasonal flowers from our garden. Above the table, high upon the wall hung a large picture of Jesus, and every Christmas morning we were lined up on the stairs, the youngest to the eldest to sing *Happy Birthday* to the picture. This was done when we had all finished our chores and breakfast had been prepared.

Christmas morning, singing happy birthday to Jesus on the stairs. Christine pulling a funny face

The children's playroom was a big room, with shelves and shelves stacked with children's books for us to read. My favourites were Enid Blyton's *Famous Five* stories. We each had our own cupboard bulging with toys and games that we'd received on our birthdays and at Christmas. Back in 1965, on the day of Winston Churchill's funeral, Auntie Hilda let us have the radio on in the playroom to listen to it. I had never heard anything so poignant; it felt as though I was actually there amongst the crowds lining the streets. It was a very sad occasion.

Halloween tea with Auntie Grace - Christine on the left with some of the other children

During Easter time we played 'hunt the egg' in the playroom; the aunties would hide lots of miniature chocolate eggs around the room, in the book cases and cupboards for us to hunt around for and if the weather was fine they would hide them around the garden for added fun. For breakfast everyone was given a brightly coloured boiled egg dyed in food colouring. On Easter Sunday every child also received an Easter egg that was put on their place at dining table at breakfast time. Easter and Christmas were always made special for us by the aunties, even though they were essentially religious times.

When one of us had a birthday, the staff would remind all the other children and they would find a suitable gift from their toy cupboard and wrap it in newspaper to be placed at the person's breakfast place. If we didn't, *'woe - betide you'* as Auntie Hilda would say. It was great because it meant we always got lots of presents, and even though they were usually things that were broken or that the other children didn't want any more, they made our birthdays special and full of excitement. I dread to think what presents the aunties must have been given on their birthdays from us kids!

Sometimes on a Saturday one or two of us kids would be left with just one or two aunties on duty, while the other aunties were on their day off and children had gone out for tea or had visitors. I remember these as being long, lonely days, where I would be left alone to amuse myself in the playroom or in the garden with Shawn, the house felt huge and empty and I couldn't wait for the others to come back from their visits so the noise and activity could start again. I hated being alone on those days.

Some children didn't have any family to visit them, or, like our mother, couldn't get to visit very often and relied on kind people, usually from the church that volunteered to take them out for day. Auntie Eve and Uncle Mike Owen were friends of Mr Jones, the headmaster from school. On hearing that we were in the orphanage, volunteered to take Christine and me twice a month on a Saturday, to their home in Patchway for tea, they had two sons of their own and we'd look forward to them all coming to pick us up. We loved spending the day with them at their house and they really spoiled us. When the weather was nice they took us out to parks and long walks through the woods. I remember a pond near to where they lived that they took us to with their sons to find tadpoles, I never failed to fall in! Auntie Eve would end up washing my clothes and wrap me up in a nice warm dressing gown while they dried. We watched their black and white television, something we didn't have at Severnleigh, we enjoyed shows like *Dr Who and the Daleks*, *Juke Box Jury* and *Thank Your Lucky Stars*. While watching telly we were given our tea, usually sandwiches, and lemonade followed by ice cream and jelly followed by lovely cream cakes. These were all special treats for us and we really looked forward to those Saturday's out with them.

Next to the playroom was the staff sitting-room, not quite as big as the children's playroom. It had large windows giving it a nice brightness and airy feeling to the whole of it. It was a calm room that was filled with music and prayer on Sundays and activity at Christmas-time. I liked being in this room.

The Staff Sitting-Room

There was a shiny black piano and a few comfy chairs dotted around the room for the aunties. Auntie Hilda had her own chair next to the bottom window facing out to the garden where she used to sit and do her knitting while we had our afternoon rest time. There was a table and chairs that we kids would sit at to write our weekly letters to our parents and pen-friends. On Sundays, when teatime was finished and cleared away, we all gathered round the piano to sing hymns while Auntie Hilda played. Students came from the theological college just a few hundred yards down the road to sing with us for an hour or so before we went to bed. Sundays comprised of a walk to Alma Road, Bethesda Church in the morning, Sunday school in the afternoon and evening service for the older ones. When Christine was a bit older, she and some of the other children were baptised at Alma Road Church in a small pool near to the pulpit, which was covered with wooden planks when not in use.

Alma Road Church

A lot of different things and activities took place in the staff-sitting room. At Christmas time we all gathered in the staff room as a big family, to open the presents that had been donated to the Muller's orphanages by generous people. A lot of work must have gone into deciding what presents would go to which home. We kids always put on a play of some sort in the sitting room for the aunties, it was usually the *Magic Tinderbox,* which, as I remember was about three cats jumping out of a match box. I remembering it being our favourite play and was probably the only one we could do well. I'm sure the aunties must have been fed up with the same old play each year, but they let us do it anyway. Every year a colossal Christmas tree was brought into the staff sitting room for us to decorate, it was so tall that us little ones put the decorations on the lower branches and the taller kids and staff covered the higher ones by using big ladders to reach the branches, by the time Mr Brooks had put the star on the top of the tree, it would be literally tipping the ceiling. Each and every one of us was involved with the decorating of it. We had lots of fun making coloured paper chains to put hang up in there and all the other downstairs rooms.

Occasionally we had 'squash evenings' in the staff sitting-room. Missionaries who had returned from countries like the Congo or Nigeria would give us a talk and slide show about the wonderful work they had done with the families over there. When I was about two years old and hadn't been living at Muller's for very long, we had an amazing visitor for tea: a small dark-haired lady named Gladys Aylewood. Miss Aylewood had been born in Edmonton on 24 February, 1902, from an early age it had been her ambition to go overseas and work as a missionary. She had studied with determination, but was turned down because her academic background was inadequate. She wasn't to be beaten and used all her savings for a passage to Yangcheng, Shanxi Province in China. For a while she worked as a foot inspector, touring the countryside to enforce the law against binding young Chinese girls. She then moved on to work with another lady named Jeannie Lawson to form '*The Inn of The Sixth Happiness*'. In 1936, she became a Chinese citizen, taking in and caring for orphans. She intervened in a volatile prison riot and advocated prison reform, risking her life many times to help those in need. The prisoners and orphans all adored her and helped to teach her their language. In 1938, the region was invaded by Japanese forces. Miss Aylewood helped and led over one hundred orphans through the mountains to safety, despite being wounded herself. In 1958, she sought to return to China following a brief return to the UK but was declined by the communist government. Instead she settled in Taiwan, where she founded the *Gladys Aylewood Orphanage,* she worked there until her demise in 1970.Gladys also has a school named after her in Edmonton England.

Once a week at Severnleigh, Auntie Betty the mending lady, who was a little old lady trying to earn a few shillings extra, came in to darn the socks and mend the boys' shorts that had been torn during the week at school, or from climbing trees. She also repaired the dresses for the girls if they had been damaged. She set up her old black *Singer* treadle sewing machine at the table in the staff room and would sew away, humming songs in her own little world. I remembered Aunty Betty as always being a happy little lady that loved to be around the children.

Every six weeks religiously, Dita the hairdresser came to cut everyone's hair in the sitting-room. I think she was the regular hairdresser for most of the Muller houses. Apart from cutting everyone's hair she would check for nits which we managed to pick up at least once a year from other kids at school. I often asked if I could grow my hair long, but, as usual the answer was no. None of us were allowed to apart from Ruth, who had always had long hair, eventually hers was cut short! Most of us had basin haircuts, which looked like Dita had plonked a basin on our head and cut round it. The boys were scalped, having unsightly short back and sides.

We also had a cleaner, Miss Bow that went around with her duster polishing everything in sight, sniffing as she went. She came in to help a couple of times a week. During holiday times like Christmas and summer another lady named Mrs Sharp would come and help her if it got too much for her on her own. At weekends and school holidays all the younger children were made to have an hour's sleep on a rug in the staff sitting-room covered by a couple of itchy blankets shared between us. It was really hard to get to sleep when we were wide awake in the light of day, especially in the summer. Quite often, I would just be dozing off and we were woken up! I guess so that we would sleep at night.

Next to the living room was the dining room, with a large fireplace that was never used, with a high mantle-piece on which Auntie Hilda kept a few beloved pieces of blue pottery she liked to collect from Devon. There were two monstrous, brown wooden dining tables with fat bulbous legs, everyone had their own place to sit at those tables at meal times and never changed the seats. We had every meal at these tables, unless it was a really nice summer's day when we'd occasionally have tea in the garden. A tall, wide window took up most of one wall, and looked out into the garden where there was a tall bird table that Mr Brooks had made. We were made to eat everything on our plate whether we liked it or not and could not leave the table until we had, we were never allowed to speak at the table during meal times unless it was to ask for something that was important so passed the meal time watching the birds scrambling after the bread that had been put out for them. The starlings were always there, but occasionally we would see robins, sparrows and thrushes. Auntie Hilda loved that.

There was a boy named George, who was always getting told off for gawping out of the window with his mouth open during meal times. At night, he often had trouble sleeping, so Auntie June would get him to do three laps around the garden to wear him out, poor George.

At the back of the dining room was a small room which was Auntie Hilda's office. All the accounts and private stuff took place in there; it was usually out of bounds to us children and was always kept locked if she wasn't in there. On Sunday evenings, the older kids were allowed in to listen to an auntie read a story such as John Bunyan's *Pilgrim's Progress*, which seemed to go on forever. The older girls could join the YSL (young sewers league) held in the office. Chris joined as soon as she was old enough and liked the fact that she could stay up a bit later.

Next to the dining room was the larder, which was always well stocked with every-thing needed for all our meals. The opened loaves of bread were always kept in a huge white stainless steel bread bin that clattered whenever the lid was removed. We never went hungry, apart from when we were naughty and were sent to eat in the playroom with bread and dripping.

In the down stairs hall was a grand staircase edged with a thick and shiny brown-wood bannister. It was held up with white spindles, although it was cleaned every day, we added extra shine to it kept it by sliding down on our bellies from top to bottom. Although this was against the rules, it was irresistible fun.

Looking up the stairs towards the landing, there was a magnificent stained-glass window that on a sunny day showed off its enchanting colours as the rays picked up the colours in the glass.

Past the kitchen, a hallway led to the back garden, laundry room and the basement. The laundry room was where Christine and I would receive phone calls from mother when she was able to ring. Sometimes Christine would be allowed into Auntie Hilda's bedroom to take the call while I was on phone in the laundry room, which meant we could have a three way conversation. I was never allowed into Auntie Hilda's room to take the calls, because according to her I snooped around. Who, me? My big sister Christine 'goody-two-shoes' told me about this in later years which made me laugh.

The entrance on the left opposite the laundry room led to the basement. It was an eerie, narrow stairway, which was daunting in the day-time let alone the dark evenings. At the bottom of the stairs, was a room with an empty coldness to it, where I would practice my piano playing ready for my up-and-coming exam. I had wanted to learn the piano for a long time, so Auntie Hilda arranged for me to have lessons on a Monday after school with a piano teacher named Mrs Rivers, she taught me well and I went on to pass my exam with a merit. Unfortunately I didn't keep my piano playing up when I got to senior school, something I regret.

Next to this room was the coal room, which contained enormous mounds of coal for the boilers. There were also numerous sacks filled with potatoes to feed us all for a couple of weeks at a time. Every Saturday we would spend a good couple of hours in that cellar, peeling pan after pan of potatoes ready for Saturday and Sunday dinners, with each of us suffering blisters on our hands. Once a month, after we had finished peeling the spuds we would have to polish every item of cutlery with Brasso silver polish until it shone - except for the wooden spoons! After this, we would set the tables for dinner at midday. Once dinner was finished and we had washed, dried and put away the all the cutlery and crockery, it would be time for the afternoon nap for an hour or so, unless we were out on a visit for the day.

The room next to the coal room had an oversized table similar to the dining tables we had in the dining room, its round bulbous legs resembled a snooker table with the top on. In this room, we polished our shoes with Auntie June's help, she was an expert and could always make them that bit shinier than us. We each had a coat hook and a cubby hole to store our shoes and wellington boots. There was a large, white, square porcelain sink where we could wash our hands after polishing our shoes, or clean our muddy boots before putting them away. Just off that room there was a small toilet and beside that a door leading up to the front garden.

In the afternoon, if we had been good children, the older girls were allowed to take us younger ones to Woolworths to spend our thru-pence pocket money. On the way back, if the weather was fine, we would go across the Downs and climb trees, walk around the woods by the gorge picking blackberries and mushrooms.

When I was around age nine, four of us kids concocted a plan to run away at midnight. As I remember, we were getting fed up of always being in trouble with Auntie Hilda; none of us seemed to be able to do anything right at that time. We grabbed what clothes we had and pulled them on over our night clothes, then crept down the huge staircase trying to dodge the one or two inevitable squeaky stairs. It would have been quieter to have slid down the bannister! We entered the larder as silently as possible so as not to wake any of the auntie's, especially Auntie Hilda who was a light sleeper, and took whatever we could carry that was edible, then stealthily tip-toed down the scary staircase to the basement cloakroom where our coats and shoes were kept. Each of us put on our coats on top of our pyjamas and clothes, looking like a Michelin Tyre. We then put our shoes on and proceeded to tip-toe out of the basement door into the dark, eerie night. There was a street light every so often, so tried to stay out of the light so as not be seen. What *were* we thinking and where the heck were we going? Just as we were nearly by the Theological College which was surrounded by trees, we panicked imagining things in the bushes watching us and shadows following us, scaring ourselves half to death. We stood dead in our tracks, all turned and looked at each other – and yelped, Eeek! Then scurried back home like scared rabbits in the dark of the night. We finally got back into our beds by doing the whole thing in reverse; incredibly we were never found out. It was a little adventure, but we never did it again. We knew where we were well off.

At the top of the main staircase, past the stained-glass window and up the six or so stairs leading to the landing, there was a sliding door which was usually left open in the day but closed at night. The first room on the left used to be the older girls' room, but in the early sixties, it was converted into a nursery for the few babies that were brought to us. Robert, Sophia and David were three babies that came to stay and it was lovely having little ones around.

On the right was Auntie Hilda's bedroom, which was totally out of bounds to everyone unless they had her permission to be in there. Next to her room there was a bathroom in which we had our daily bath every evening, mostly sharing the same bath water. The bathroom had three sinks so we were able to get washed for school without getting in each other's way. We had our own place for our toothbrush along with the disgusting block of Gibbs toothpaste that left an unpleasant gritty taste in my mouth. Next to the bathroom was my bedroom, with nursery rhyme wallpaper featuring Little Bo Peep, Humpty Dumpty and many more popular characters. On summer evenings the sun's rays would shine through the curtains and I could never seem to get to sleep, so I would imagine the nursery rhyme characters coming to life and creeping around the walls. Sometimes I'd end up imagining horrible things, scaring myself and hide my head under the covers till it went away.

I shared this room with four others, one of whom was my sister Christine, until she was old enough to be moved upstairs with the older girls. Ruth's bed was on the left hand side on entering the room next to a big old black fireplace surrounded by cast iron mantels. Stood In front of it was a large chest of drawers, on it Christine and I kept a beautiful black and white framed photo of our mother looking just like the Queen.

My mother - 1960

Paul, Ruth's brother slept on the other side of the fireplace. The other girl in our room was Jackie; her bed was opposite Paul's. She was from either Kenya or Nigeria I think? Jackie's mum, on her visits would usually bring a tub of Astral cream for the dry skin she would suffer with on her elbows and knees. It was a luxury to have things like that, and I would often ask Jackie if I could have some because I loved the smell and texture. Our bedtime was 6.30p.m and the aunties took it in turns to sit on the landing until we had all gone to sleep to making sure there was no talking. There were a number of times when I was caught messing about. I'd hear Christine giggling under her covers while I'd be doing headstands on my bed, showing all my glory with my winceyette nightie round my neck, thinking the auntie on the landing had gone downstairs. Wrong! I'd be caught in the act, bent over the end of the bed and walloped with a wooden hair brush on my bare bottom. It did hurt, but did I learn? No, I carried on doing those headstands and I carried on getting caught!

My bedroom in the middle of the picture

Every weekday morning, we were woken up at six o'clock prompt. At weekends, we had a lie-in for an extra hour. Our clean clothes for the next day had been set out the night before on the top of each of our lockers. We were each responsible for the making of our own beds and when we'd finished, our beds were checked to make sure we had made it properly with hospital corners and put the counterpane back neatly without a crease on it.

Every Thursday, we had to change our sheets in the morning, so we were woken a bit earlier on that particular day. Once again, one of the aunties or older girls would come in and check we had all made our beds perfectly. One of the older girls liked to show her authority by bullying us around in the mornings. None of us ever breathed a word to the aunties as we were scared we would get in trouble for lying, which meant your mouth washed out with soap or a teaspoon of mustard. Guess who hates mustard now - Christine!

Along the corridor on the right was the boys' room, shared by George, Keith and Arthur. I don't know how they got on at night, but I do know nearly every evening one of the boys from that room would need to use the toilet after the auntie on duty had gone downstairs. It was a short way along a narrow corridor from their room to the toilet and we girls would giggle under our covers as we could hear him scurrying down the corridor breaking wind. This particular boy was a comical young lad, who always seemed to have a runny nose. When he wore his long grey socks, one was usually falling down round his ankles. Just a little memory I have of him that makes me smile.

Off the landing on the right hand side was a flight of stairs, leading to the other aunties' and the older girls' rooms. We young ones were never allowed to go up there, although I did go up now and again when Christine was older and had moved out of my bedroom. If I had been caught, I would probably have got the wooden spoon and accused of 'hobnobbing' (another one of Auntie Hilda's favourite expressions) with the older girls.

Chapter 8
MARRIED

On 18 March, 1958, my mother wrote to Mrs Horne.

Dear Mrs Horne,
Thank-you for letting me know the new address of the children. I
hope they will be happy in their new home. I am afraid I will not be
able to come and see them next visiting day as I have just started
a new job here in a Publican Hotel and Easter will be very busy,
but my day off is on Tuesdays, would it be possible for me to
come on that day? All the children have holidays for Easter as
perhaps yours do, please let me know if this will be convenient or
not. The Tuesday following Easter Sunday will be convenient. My
new job is not too bad, only very tiring, still, I am happy enough for
the present. Trusting you are well I will close, oh and by the way I
heard from Middlesbrough Court, they had sent the money but did
not say how much, could you let me know as I have to keep check
on Mr Warrior in case he gets in arrears.
God bless you
Very sincerely yours
P N Warrior

Muller's didn't approve of my mother's new job and on 19
March, 1958, Mrs Horne wrote:

Dear Mrs Warrior,
Thank you for your letter telling me about your new post. I am
sorry that you have taken one in a licensed Hotel as it does not
sound a very nice sort of job not as though you would be working
amongst people who would be much help to you.
It will be quite alright for you to come and visit the children on
Tuesday April the 8th as this is holiday time and Christine will be
home from school. I have told Miss Ashton, their housemother that
you will come that day.
This of course is a special arrangement, but in the ordinary way
will you arrange to keep to the proper visiting Saturday as it is so
inconvenient for the staff if visitors come on all sorts of different

days. If you have any difficulty in arranging this, then I will write to your employer for you, and we always find that people are most considerate in allowing the mother to be free to visit her children on the proper day.
With all good wishes
Yours sincerely
Mrs Horne

Muller's were a religious organisation and working in a public house where alcohol was served, was totally frowned upon in those days. Needless to say, they were not very happy with my mother's choice of work and did not think it was a stable environment to be bringing her children into as she would be spending all sorts of hours in the evenings out working.

On 29 March, 1958, my mother wrote from Sibley Grove, East Ham.

Dear Mrs Horne,
Thank you for your letter, as you will see I have changed my address. I have found through my new friends at work a really nice comfortable room of my own with every convenience and most of all its clean, the last place was not so. The people were nice but the place itself was not clean. I think now I am really settled. I hope nothing happens to spoil my good luck, I pray to god every night that he stays by my side. My job is working out very nicely, and the manager and his wife are very helpful and he says I can come and see the children as arranged; it is only because we are so busy at holidays like Easter that I can't ask him as he is being so good to me.
I have my middle brother in hospital in London and he is very poorly, the manager has helped me to go and see him as often as possible, so you see they are not too bad. I have two very good friends here who have two children of their own. I made friends with them at the garage so you see perhaps I will soon get on my feet once again and have a new life and make a home for the children really worthwhile. I would like to see you when I come

down and talk with you. Will it be possible? Please let me know at
your own convenience.
Sincerely yours
Mrs P N Warrior.

On 31 March, 1958, Mrs Horne replied:

Dear Mrs Warrior,
Just a line to thank you for your letter and to let you know that it
will be quite convenient for you to come in and see me on
Tuesday morning April 8th, before you see the children
Yours sincerely
Mrs Horne

Left to right: Christine, Paul and me in the garden of Severnleigh

My mother managed to come and see us. She took us into Bristol city centre to have lunch by the fountain on the rooftop of Lewis's shopping store, our favourite place.

After lunch she took us on to the Downs to have a run around and play. We rolled in the grass and climbed trees. As we walked along the Downs holding her hand she would always be singing, I asked her why she was always singing and she replied, 'Because I'm happy to be with my darling girls.' She was happy with us and we were happy to be with her. Christine and I missed her dreadfully would be heartbroken on the occasions she didn't turn up or couldn't make the visit. At times we both desperately longed for a visit from her.

A couple of times my mother took us to the zoo where we rode on Rosie, the famous elephant who was there for years. All the children would walk along-side her waiting for their turn to have a ride on her.

hant, seen here giving rides to young childr
along the main promenade

Janet and Derek Fisher - 'Bygone Bristol' Books

If the weather was nice, which it mostly was in those days, we'd sometimes have a picnic on the Downs; we so loved just being with her, it was such a treat for us.

On 24 April, 1958, mother wrote from Victoria Rd Middlesbrough

Dear Mrs Horne,
I must let you know I've arrived back home for a week or two as my father is very sick, and my mother is very ill and waiting to go under an operation, so I may not get to see the children next week. So would you break it to them? If I do not manage to get down to see them I shall of course send them a parcel to make up a little for it. I will let you know later how things are.
I shall write to Christine.
Sincerely yours

P N Warrior

On 26 April, 1958, Mrs Horne wrote:

Dear Mrs Warrior,
I am sorry to hear of you parents illness; I do hope your mother
will come through her operation successfully and that both of them
will soon be better. They must be very thankful that you are able
to come and look after them in this trouble.
We will certainly explain to the children and tell them you will
come another day as soon as you can manage it. Thank you for
letting us know in good time so that the children do not have to
expect you and be disappointed.
Yours sincerely
Mrs Horne.

We were now into the month of May and my mother was trying her best to hold down a job but desperately trying to get a Saturday off at the beginning of the month so she could come and see us. Meanwhile, we were settled in at Severnleigh; I had had my second birthday, and Christine was going to be five in July and due to start school in September.

On 13 May, 1958, my mother wrote from Sibley Grove, East Ham.

Dear Mrs Horne,
I must at first apologise for taking too long to answer your letter. I
have arrived back here and found I have lost my job, so now I
must get another one. My mother had her operation yesterday but
is still poorly. My father is not too well. I would have stayed at
home but there are problems with other family members and I
think my dad has enough to cope with. I do hope that the children
are well and were not too disappointed at not seeing me, I really
missed seeing them, I will write to them. I have seen a lot of
Linda's father the past couple of months and he wants me to
marry him and save up for a home for the children, he really does
think a terrible lot about me and worships the children. I told him I
would let him know next time he is home what I have decided.

Well Mrs Horne that seems to be all for the present, excepting
there has been no money paid into the court by Mr Warrior as he
is on the sick, everything seems to happen all at once.
Cheerio and god bless you
Mrs P N Warrior.

On 15 May, 1958, Mrs Horne wrote:

Dear Mrs Warrior,
I just want to write to you with reference to what you say about
Linda's father and his wish to marry you. Do be careful what you
do, and make no promises in a hurry. You have gone through so
much trouble with these two men and it would be dreadful if you
committed yourself to this and then it turns out unhappily. There is
no need to rush into anything for the children's sake as you know
they are cared for and happy, and it would be far better for your
sake and theirs that you go slowly and do nothing rash.
It would be a lovely thing if you could set up a real Christian home,
such as we try to give these children, but unless you can do that it
is far better to leave things as they are.
Yours sincerely
Mrs Horne.

On 6 June, 1958, my mother wrote:

Dear Mrs Horne,
I am hoping to come and see the children on Saturday. I have only
just started my new job in a small restaurant, it's a nice job and I
get all my meals included but my wage is only four pounds per
week, so by the time I have finished paying my way I have very
little left. I have sent to Middlesbrough to see if there is any money
in the court yet, if that comes through I shall let you know by
Saturday morning whether I shall be able to come through or not. I
do long to see the children so very much trusting they are well. I
hope to see you soon.
Sincerely
Mrs P N Warrior.

The next time my mother wrote to Mrs Horne was near the end of the month, so I don't think she had made the last visit.

This is the letter of 23 June, 1958.

Dear Mrs Horne,
I feel I must write at the moment, you see after reading your letter I understand what you were trying to convey to me and please accept my heartfelt thanks, I appreciate your understanding. I want mostly to make a happy Christian home for the children, you know I have their interest to heart. What I am trying to say is I am getting married to Mr Norris, Linda's father and would sincerely like your blessing. Of course I have thought it all over and realise it's a big step to take, but I am convinced I am doing the right thing.
It will take a long time to get a home where we can have the children but I wouldn't want to move them until I have my own house and we can all be happy together again.
I should like to see you next time I come to visit the children, we can talk much better than by letter, so if it's permissible I will come to Ashley Down with the children on the afternoon as it is always lunchtime when I arrive at Bristol. Trusting you are well I shall say God bless you until we meet again.
Yours Very Sincerely
Mrs P N Warrior

On 25 June, 1958, Mrs Horne wrote:

Dear Mrs Warrior,
I am not sure whether I do right to still call you this? You have not given me a different address so I hope this will reach you in any case.
I must accept what you say of having thought over carefully what you are doing, and do most sincerely trust that things will turn out happily. You say you want to make a Christian home for your children, and you know the way to do this is to make sure you understand what it is to be a Christian yourself. You know the way

to God through faith in the Lord Jesus Christ, and if you accept him simply as your saviour, and try to go in his way, then your home will be a Christian one.
I should be very glad for you to come and see me, as you suggest, when you visit the children on July 5th. We have moved to new offices, as you will see you can get here very easily on a Number two bus from outside Temple Meads Station to the Homeopathic Hospital. From there you walk down to Cotham Lawn Rd, which is just opposite the bus stop, Cotham Park is on your right at the end of that road. You should either come here first or after you have collected the children, whichever you like. The children are very well and will be delighted to see you.
Yours Sincerely
Mrs Horne.

My mother didn't get to see us on Saturday 5 July.
On 10 July, 1958, she wrote:

Dear Mrs Horne,
I must first apologize for not letting you know I couldn't get to see the children, but the doctor advised me not to, as I have or say, still got a very bad dose of septic tonsillitis. I do suffer every year. Perhaps when I am up and alright again you would let me see the children. I did miss coming, I had looked forward to it so very much. I love the snaps I took last time I was there.
You will see I have changed my address; it is only temporary until I get myself a proper place. My husband has returned to sea, it may be months before I see him again, but when he comes home we hope to buy our little home and make a new life ahead.
Please write to me Mrs Horne. I feel so miserable at being ill and missing seeing the children.
God Bless you, also Christine and Linda

Mrs P N Norris.
(My mother was now married to my dad and her name changed to Norris)

On 11 July, 1958, Mrs Horne wrote:

Dear Mrs Norris,
I am sorry to hear how poorly you have been and do hope you will soon be much better.
You can certainly arrange to come and see the children another Saturday as you were not able to come on visiting day.
When you have to disappoint them like this, would you either ring up or send a telegram so that they may not be expecting you. They were all dressed up and waiting for you on Saturday and nobody knew what had happened and why you did not come, so they did feel rather let down. They are very well and enjoying as much time as possible during this lovely weather out in the garden.
Yours Sincerely
Mrs Horne.

Auntie June had taken Christine and I out to a tea room at the top of Blackboy Hill the afternoon mother couldn't visit us. This was no doubt to make us feel better as we were feeling sad and disappointed at my mother's non-appearance.

Chapter 9

THE BREAK UP

My mother's marriage to my dad wasn't going to well at all; she states that she had really only married him to get a home so that Christine and I could leave the orphanage. In October 1958, my mother wrote to Auntie Hilda to let her know she couldn't get to see us again.

Dear Miss Ashton,
Just a line to let you know I will not be coming down next Saturday and I want to save my fare for the children's Christmas presents. I hardly have enough wages at the moment to get all I'd like to for them, but can you give me some idea of what they would really like. I think Christine mentioned a doll. Please find out for me. Regarding our conversation, I have not seen my husband though he has docked in Glasgow. I think he is getting an annulment because I refused to be his wife. Perhaps it is just as well, as I did only marry him for the children. I have no feelings for him and we would never be happy, he wants Linda and has told me so. I often wonder if I should have let him have her, she would have a real home and never wanted for anything. Anyway I shall see you when I next come. I really do enjoy talking to you and feel better for it. Give my love to both children.

Sincerely yours.
Mrs P N Norris

PS: I am going to miss my visit very much.

Christine and I had been in Severnleigh for nearly a year and there wasn't any sign that we would be leaving in the near future. Things weren't getting any better for mother! She was in and out of jobs, feeling unsettled and employers not giving her time off to visit us, all this added to her hardship.

On 1 November, 1958, Muller's wrote:
Dear Mrs Norris,

I was very sorry indeed to read the letter Miss Ashton passed onto me from you and to learn how unhappy things are between you and your husband at present. I was also greatly disturbed at your suggestion that you might take little Linda away and hand her over to your husband's people. This would be a terrible break for the child and Christine would be heart-broken if they had to part. I do hope that you will do nothing in a hurry but will come and discuss things with me before coming to a decision.
The children are well and happy and now enjoying their half term holiday.
Yours sincerely
Mrs Horne.

On Bonfire night, 5 November, 1958, my mother wrote:

Dear Mrs Horne,
Thank you for your letter received on the 3rd November. It was most kind of you to write and please do not worry over me doing anything silly regarding the children. I have always tried to do what is best for them and will continue to do so in the future. I did fully believe I was doing the right thing when I married my husband, but as you are probably aware by now it was quite the opposite. I believe God has a reason for all the rights and wrongs and I trust him to help me to do what is the right thing now. He is my only saviour.
Please give my love to the children when you see them again and once again thank you and god bless.
Yours sincerely
Mrs P N Norris.

November 5th was the yearly Bonfire Night event held at the Bristol Rovers football ground. This amazing firework display which was held once every year would always arouse much excitement amongst the adults and the children. The auntie's, uncles and children from all of the Muller's Homes went to this event. In my very early years I was too young to appreciate it, but as I grew older, I really enjoyed being part of this event. The fireworks were incredible, they lit high up in the sky with blue, green, yellow, red and white showers of sparkles and loud bangs that made us jump out of our skin. The best was always saved for last and at the very end, the show finished with a depiction of the Queen and Prince Philip. That was the most amazing part of the whole show! One year, I was naughty. I don't remember what I had done, but as a punishment, my privileges were taken away from me. I had to stay at home and was sent to bed after eating bread and dripping while all the other kids went off to enjoy the fun. I made sure that didn't happen again.

A man named Robert Bennet was the organiser of the firework displays, known to all as 'Uncle Bob'. He worked for The Bristol Evening Post and in later years worked for BBC Radio Bristol. He was the father of the late Radio Bristol presenter Roger Bennett. He was a caring and considerate man of many talents. Soon after the Evening Post Newspaper was founded in the nineteen thirties, Uncle Bob set up a selection in the newspaper for children named 'The Pillar Box Club'. Through this, he arranged for thousands of children to write to Pen Friends around the world. He was a cartoonist who created the characters 'Freddie the Funny Photographer' and 'Reggie the Rotten Reporter'. As well as this, he helped with various charities by collecting milk bottle tops and silver paper – I'm not entirely sure what they were saved for though? I do remember us saving them for his charity while living in Severnleigh though. He organised Christmas parties for the less fortunate and the homes like ours this enabled us to meet other kid's from different homes. Uncle Bob was also an accomplished jazz musician and was well known for leading the Blue Notes Jazz Band by playing the soprano saxophone and clarinet.

Uncle Bob

Severnleigh also had our own bonfire night to be held on the nearest Saturday to the 5th November. We all had fun in the weeks leading up to bonfire night, gathering things for our own bonfire in our big garden. However small or tall we were we all contributed with the building of it on a waste area near the vegetable patch. It was a great way to clear up the garden of branches and twigs that had fallen during the autumn. Everything and anything went onto that fire; we would even pick things up from the downs on the way home from school to put on it. We made a Guy Fawkes to sit at the top of it, with the help of Mr Brooks of course. On the actual day, aunties made toffee apples, warm drinks and sandwiches for everyone and of course we all had a couple of sparklers each. Poor Shawn was scared half to death by the noise of the fireworks and needed to be comforted in the house when Mr Brooks lit them. Before lighting the bonfire, we all went around it to check that no hedgehogs or any other of God's Creatures had hidden under it. When we were sure as we could be that it was clear, Mr Brooks lit it. We were well supervised and kept safe at all times while watching the fire roar into the sky. They were fun times and great childhood memories for me.

It was approaching Christmas, an exciting time as usual when we all enjoyed helping with the decorating of the Christmas tree and the house. There were parties and presents for us all to enjoy. There was also the singing of Christmas carols in the staff sitting room with our extended family from the Theological College just yards down the road, the church services and lots more. It was such a lovely time, and I so loved it when the house was filled with music.

Chapter 10

A NEW BEGINNING

1958 had been and gone. I was coming up to my fourth birthday in February. My mother had had a rethink about what she was going to do. She needed stability, without it she was never going to get us back. She decided she was going to join the WRAF (*Women's Royal Air Force*) so she wrote to Mrs Horne at Muller's with information about her new plans.

On 11 February, 1959

Dear Mrs Horne,

I do hope you are all well. I know the children are as I had a very nice letter from Miss Ashton on Friday last, she does think an awful lot of all the children, it makes me happy to know they are all happy and loved as well as being cared for.
I don't know if Miss Aston mentioned it or not, but I told her I would like to go in the W.R.A.F as I would have more advantages for learning a trade and would be able to save regularly, and be able to spend more time with the children when on leave without having to worry about getting the sack from my jobs, and wondering if I can afford the fare to Bristol. Being in the forces we are granted so many free passes.
I had an interview with the commanding officer and it seems I have passed my tests, but they would like a letter from you verifying that I signed my name on your application form for the children to be in your care until they are fifteen or as such times that my circumstances change, it seems they want proof that I haven't only recently parted with the children but over twelve months ago. I got permission from Mr Norris to go in the forces, now he has gone abroad, so I have to make a new start to do something really worthwhile and I feel this is the opportunity I need to prove I can be of some use, and to save for my own home in the future years. I shall sign on for five years if I am accepted, so if you feel I am doing right would you write to the address enclosed.

I know in my own heart I should have done this before then I would not have married Mr Norris. I have always been keen to go in the forces to learn and be of some use and able to hold my head and say I am able to work. As it is now I have no real trade behind me and when I'm interviewed for a job they won't listen because I have never been able to hold a situation for more than a year, so please help me to do what I would like to do. I am really keen and interested in this life and if I am given the chance I shall be able to make a new start.

It is very hard to explain my feelings on paper but I pray you can understand what I have tried to say.

I hope that I will personally hear from you, also I would like to very much.

God bless you and guide you as he is guiding me. I know in my heart that he is with me all the time.

Yours sincerely

Mrs P N Norris.

On 13 February, 1959, this letter came from Muller's to my mother:

Dear Mrs Norris,

I have written to the W.R.A.F Commanding Officer as you ask, just a short note confirming what you say about the children.

Whatever you decide to do in the future I do beg of you to keep the children in mind and try to lead the sort of life that you know will be the right example to them.

It is a good thing that you have them to think of and not only yourself, and I trust that their unconscious influence will go on being a help to you.

We shall try to bring them up to know and love the Lord Jesus and to follow in his ways. You know this way too and if you would sincerely put your trust in him you would find the strength you need to lead the sort of life that you know to be right.

Do let me know how things go with you, and continue to write regularly to the children wherever you are.

Yours sincerely

Mrs Horne.

The short note to the WRAF Commanding Officer from Muller's read:

Dear Madam,
I write to confirm that the two children of Mrs P N Norris were received into these Homes in December of 1957 as their mother was unable to provide for them.
She understood at the time that the children are only received here who need a long term placing, and we are willing to keep them as long as necessary.
Yours faithfully
Muller Homes for Children

The new beginning was not to be. My mother was not accepted in the WRAF. It wasn't clear why she was refused but assumed it was because her children were under the age of fifteen. She had returned back to square one looking for suitable employment where she could get the first Saturday free each month. Feeling very disappointed she decided to move back with her mother (Nana Smith) in Redcar, Yorkshire.

While living at Nana's, mother went through various different jobs, shop work and serving petrol in a garage, just trying to earn what she could and get some stability in her life, but again struggled to get a first Saturday in each month off for visits to see us. She couldn't settle and ultimately she left for London again. At least she would be a bit nearer Bristol. She found work in The Old Tavern pub in Chingford, London, but once again due to the working hours this meant she couldn't get the first Saturday off to visit us.

As a friend had offered a lift to Bristol on Sunday 9 June 1959, she accepted the kind offer and turned up to see us.
Mrs Horne was not happy about this and wrote to my mother.

Dear Mrs Norris,

Just a note to you with reference to your last visit to the children, you do know that the first Saturday in each month is the right day for visiting, and if you are quite unable to come on that day the House Parent will make other arrangements for you to see them, but you must write to her beforehand.
If you consider the matter for a moment from our point of view you will realise how very awkward it would be for House Mothers if all parents turned up at all sorts of odd times expecting to visit the children.
We should prefer you keep to a Saturday. In any case as that is the day that other children have visitors, and a school day is not very convenient.
If you have any difficulty in coming on a Saturday I will write to your employer officially, and we have always found they are most understanding about making an arrangement for a Mother to visit her children.
I gather that you have not after all joined the W.R.A.F and wonder what happened about this. I shall be pleased to hear how you are getting on.
Yours sincerely
Mrs Horne.

My mother replied on 12 June, 1959.

Dear Mrs Horne,
Many thanks for your letter. I am very sorry if I upset you over my visit to see the children. I do fully realise that Saturday is the visiting day, but having the chance of a lift to Bristol I took it. I had not seen the children in six months so therefore I naturally thought it would be overlooked for once. I have mostly kept to visiting Saturdays. I think I have only once before been on a week day and that was when I took the Christmas toys. So please accept my apologies for not arranging something first. I know it is impossible for me to get a Saturday off in this job as Saturday and Sunday are the very busiest days. We do such a lot of brunches. I am not wholly satisfied with this job and am intending to change it shortly. I have an interview with a manager of a new garage opening in a week or two. I have explained to him I should like to

have a Saturday off to visit my children, he understood and said it
can be arranged so I think everything might turn out for the best.
I meant to tell you about the W.R.A.F as soon as I settled down
somewhere.
I don't know why I was turned down? I can only assume it was
because the children were under fifteen years. They are not
supposed to accept anyone with children under this age. I was
very disappointed of course but its Gods way and I accept it.
Please don't write to my employers, they have no children and
therefore don't realise what it means to me to see mine. I showed
them your letter but all I got was " how can you expect to have a
Saturday off " unquote. I shall let you know immediately I change
my situation because my address will change also.
Trusting you are well and I hope to hear from you soon. God Bless
you
Very Sincerely Yours
Mrs P N Norris

On holiday in Minehead, 1959

August 1959.

It was the school summer holidays and every year we
Muller's children would go on holiday to the seaside. Usually we
would join up with children from other Muller homes. This year we

went to Minehead, as usual we had a lovely time; we went to the beach and as always, managed to drop my sandwiches in the sand and had to eat gritty ham and tomato, cheese and tomato and egg and cress sandwiches. Some days, the aunties took us to a large outdoor pool with a big fountain in the shallow end. I loved splashing around in there. Summers were hot in those days so the aunties made sure we all had plenty of suntan protection on. However, I still managed to blister on my shoulders from the sun. One year quite badly during a holiday in Bournemouth.

On 27 August, 1959, my mother sent Muller's her new address – Frankland Road, Chingford. Mrs Horne replied:

Dear Mrs Norris,
We have just heard from Middlesbrough Magistrates Court that the reason we have received no money from Mr Warrior for Christine since February last year (1958) is that he has not paid in the full amount of two pounds per week, which was to be a pound for you and a pound for Christine, but that he has paid a total of 15 pounds of which you have taken the full amount.
As you have not made any contributions for the children and have not had the expense of keeping them, we are wondering why you have done this. You can of course take proceedings against Mr Warrior in the matter.
Christine and Linda will be returning from their holiday from Minehead tomorrow where they have had the most delightful time.
Yours sincerely
Mrs Horne

Holiday in Minehead - Auntie June made these swimming costumes for us

On 16 September, 1959, my mother wrote to Muller's.

Dear Mrs Horne,
I hope you will forgive the delay in answering your letter but I have been trying to get a few days off work to go up home and sort things out. I did not realize Mr Warrior had let the maintenance slide as much as you say it has. I would also not have drawn the money I did when I was out of work. You say I have not been supporting the children, but I have been saving a few shillings a week to provide some clothing for them hoping I would save some expense. I have tried to work my expenses out and will try to send whatever I can per month hoping it will help towards the upkeep of my two little girls. My wages amount to six pounds ten shillings per week, and I will try to save some so I can visit the children regularly, there are also my own expenses to pay. I do hope you will forgive me for not realizing before now the responsibility which I do owe you. If I can manage to get a few days off work I shall go north and see about a court order, but I am afraid I shall have to forfeit my next visit to the children unless any of my friends are coming to Bristol.
Yours sincerely
Mrs P N Norris.

PS. I have just received notice I can have this weekend off to go up to Middlesbrough.

On 28 September, my mother wrote:

Dear Mrs Horne,
Just a line to let you know I was up at Middlesbrough last week end and I have taken out a summons against Mr Warrior. He will be up at court on the 12th October for arrears. I shall of course let you know the results as soon as I hear.
Trusting everyone is in good health and God bless you for being so good and patient.
Very sincerely yours
Mrs P N Norris.

Chapter 11

SCHOOL?

On 17 November, 1959, Mrs Horne from Muller's wrote to the education officer about me starting school.

Dear Sir,
This little girl, who is in our care, lives in our home at 1, Stoke Hill, Bristol 9, and is due to start school in February of next year. She is a well-developed healthy child, quick and intelligent and would be quite ready to go to school at the beginning of next term if permission can be given for this. Mr Welsh, the Headmaster at St John's Junior mixed and Infant school is willing to admit her at the beginning of term but requires your permission as she will not be five years old at that date.
I shall be glad to know whether you would think it in order for her to start school at the beginning of next term.
Yours faithfully
Mrs Horne

On 19 November, 1959, the education officer replied to Mrs Horne.

Dear Madam,
Linda Warrior, 26. 2. 55
Thank you for your letter of 17th November.
I regret that the committee are strictly limited in the number of children for which they may provide education below the age of five years and unless there are especially difficult circumstances which you would like the committee to consider in this case, it will not be possible for me to arrange for Linda to begin school before the normal time.
Yours faithfully
Chief Education Officer.

On 23 November, 1959 Muller's wrote to Mr Welsh, the headmaster of St John's School

Dear Mr Welsh,
I have now heard from the chief Education Officer regretting that
he cannot give permission for Linda to start school at the
beginning of next term as she will not yet be five, unless there are
especially difficult circumstances which we would like his
committee to consider. As this is not the case we shall have to
leave it and assume she could enter at half term.
With many thanks for willingness to help.
Yours sincerely
Muller's

Mr Welsh's reply:

Dear Mrs Horne,
Re-Linda Warrior 26. 2. 55
Thank you for your letter of the 23rd instant. We regret that we are
unable to admit Linda after half- term, as new admissions are only
taken at the beginning of a term.
Linda will, therefore be eligible to attend St John's at the
commencement of the summer term – 2nd May 1960.
Yours sincerely
Mr Welsh.

So that was that for a while. I carried on being cared for by the aunties in Severnleigh without school. My very early years are a bit vague and I really don't remember what I did with my days, so I have relied on my sister Christine and also Auntie June to help my recollection of those times. I do remember I was well cared for and the fabulous holidays I had in Bournemouth, Weston-Super-Mare and Minehead with the other children. This was in addition to Christmases, Easters, birthdays and Bonfire Nights. While we were having all the fun, I'm sure my mother was too, but she was still trying to make ends meet the best way she could.

Chapter 12

A NEW FRIEND

On 30 November, 1959, my mother wrote to Auntie Hilda.

My dear Miss Aston,
Many thanks for your letter and wishing me well. Since my last
letter to you I've had Influenza and what a dose, I have been so ill
and I'm still recovering now. I hope to be well enough to visit the
children on Saturday week.
Also I have not mentioned it before, but I have been going out with
a boy here for the last five months, and both he and his family
have been very good to me. I would like to bring him with me to
meet Christine and Linda. Do you think it will be alright? I would
like him to meet them but I would also like your approval first, he
knows all there is to know about me and appreciates that I told
him all about me instead of lying to him; he is a good honest boy
and so are his family. There are quite a few of them in his family
and have accepted me for knowing me. I feel quite happy with all
my friends, and someday I hope that I will have a happy Christian
home of my own with my two girls by my side. Also, I hope to see
you next time I come to visit although I think you mentioned being
away; I do so look forward to seeing you on my visits.
I hope to hear from you soon, and by the way we are bringing the
children's Christmas presents next week, will it be ok?
Cheerio for now and God Bless you and my love to the girls.
Sincerely yours
Phyllis Norris.

Auntie Hilda was away at the time, so mother's letter to her
was re-directed to an address in Salisbury Green, Southampton
where Auntie Hilda was staying at that time. Auntie Hilda wrote a
letter to Mrs Horne, enclosing the letter my mother had written.

Dear Mrs Horne,
I am enclosing a letter which arrived yesterday which was re-
directed from Bristol written by Linda and Christine's mother. You

will see what she says about bringing yet another man into their lives that knowing what your wishes would be in these peculiar circumstances, am asking you, please, if you will be so good to deal with this for me. Linda already prays "Please bless my two Daddies!" maybe in the future it will be THREE! I will write to Mrs Warrior (Norris) and tell her you will be letting her know about Saturday. Here's hoping you are well, and that no one has been washed away with all the floods we have been having!
Yours sincerely
Hilda M Ashton.

On 1 December, 1959, Mrs Horne wrote to my mother.

Dear Mrs Norris,
Miss Aston has passed on your letter as she was not sure how she had better handle your request.
I shall be glad if you will come here to the office to see me next Saturday before you go to visit the children. Bring your friend if you wish.
It is quite easy to get here either from Temple Meads Station or from the Coach Station. From Temple Meads you take a number twenty bus as far as the Homeopathic Hospital and walk down Cotham Lawn Rd and turn right at the end onto Cotham Park. From the Coach Station you take a number hundred and forty five bus to Freemantle Rd. From the end of this road turn left up Cotham Brow and Cotham Park turns off on the right.
I am usually in the office all day on visiting Saturday to see parents, so there is no need for you to make an appointment as to the time you will get here.
Yours sincerely
Mrs Horne.

Meanwhile Mrs Horne wrote another letter on 2 December, 1959, to the chief education officer regarding me starting school.

Dear Sir,
Thank you for your letter of November 19th explaining that Linda cannot be admitted to school at the beginning of next term.

I cannot pretend that there are any especially difficult circumstances which would warrant this.
We would have liked her to go as she is an intelligent child and longing to get to school, but we understand that she must wait until the following term.
Yours faithfully
Mrs Horne.

Christmas was a busy time and either through lack of funds or not being able to get time off work, mother didn't get to visit us on the allocated visiting day. She wrote from Frankland Road, London to see if she could come on another day.

Dear Mrs Norris,
Miss Ashton has passed on your message to me about visiting the children tomorrow and calling to see me.
We should be so glad if you would keep it in mind that the first Saturday in each month is the official visiting day and then I am in the office to meet parents who wish to see me. I cannot see you tomorrow as I have to be in our Weston Houses and the following Saturday down in Minehead House.
We will arrange for you to see the children tomorrow this time, but it is most inconvenient to have these continual alterations of the proper arrangement.
I am sorry if I seem unkind about this, I have so often reminded you that the first Saturday is the day to come. If you consider how many children and parents we deal with and try to help, you will realise what difficulties it would make if a number of them continually wanted special arrangements.
Linda has been rather poorly and under the doctor, but she is better now.
If you want to see me perhaps you could arrange to come next month on the first Saturday, which will be March the 5th and I will be glad to see you.
Yours sincerely
Mrs Horne
My mother visited as regularly as she could, but it was disappointing for us when she didn't turn up on visiting days, it

made my heart sink and I felt so sad. It was hard to understand being a child, especially as she wasn't allowed to come on another day. Sometimes, it was months before she could get to see us.

In the summer, we went on holiday for two weeks to Bournemouth with children from the other scattered homes. We would stay in one of the big old house that Muller's had. The dining room was enormous with long tables and benches we sat at to eat, all in a long, neat row facing each other. This helped us to get to know the other children from different homes. The garden was massive with slides and climbing frames surrounded by tall trees, we played rounders and skipping games just having a lovely time. The summer was really warm and sometimes we got sunburnt on the beach as we did in Weston-Super-Mare. In the early evenings after tea the Aunties took us out for long walks along the sea front and surrounding areas. It was always an anti-climax when we had to go back to Severnleigh at the end of our holiday, but there was always next year to look forward to.

Chapter 13

SCHOOL YEARS

Janet and Derek Fisher - 'Bygone Bristol' Books,

The 'Top School' 2002

September, 1960

My first day at school and part of the routine was to stand in line with all the other school-age children for our everyday table-spoon of malt before we left the house. I hated that stuff, but, it was good for me they said! One of the Aunties took me to school

106

for my first day. I was told in my later years that I cried, but don't most kids on their first day.

My first school, the Top School, was an attractive building with a beautiful, tiled roof, standing in all its brilliance at the top of Blackboy Hill. The school had a high wall all around it, and the main gate led to a zebra crossing where a regular lollipop-man saw us across the road safely every morning and afternoon. He knew each and every one of us kids by name and always asked after any child who was absent.

Built in 1851 and known as The Top School because of its position at the top of Blackboy Hill, it housed the infant classes and the first year junior classes. The toilets in school were located on the far side of the playground and were so cold, especially in the winter time.

The Annexe was the junior part of the school and was formerly known as Anglesea Place Board School. In the olden days, long before my time there, the boys used the Worrall Road entrance to the juniors, and the girls and infants used the Anglesea Place entrance. The boys and girls were kept completely separate and never met during school time. I read that an elderly ex-pupil had once been sent to the headmaster to be punished for speaking to her brother on the stone steps leading to the boy's school.

The name later changed to 'The Annexe of St John's Junior Mixed and Infants School' only three classes of children were taught there: the second, third and fourth year juniors. Access was then from a door in Worrall Road and down stone steps into the small tarmac playground. When it rained everyone went under the arches, the roof of which was the Hall floor.

Every term, the infants and juniors went to a school service in St John's Church, then later to All Saints, Clifton. At Christmas, the juniors went up to the Top School to put on a special production for the infants. In 1977, The Annexe was knocked down and rebuilt in modern red bricks, all apart from the listed part of the front wall and the Arches. It was reopened on 29 March, 1979.

107

The listed side view of the Annexe

The listed front of the Annexe

The Arches at the Annexe

I made a few friendships in my infant years that continued through my junior years: One such friend was Jonathan, who remained my best friend until I left in 1966. Catherine Nicholls was one of my classroom friends, we both loved gymnastics and were in fact, fairly good at it. We would spend more time on our hands than our feet walking the length of the playground and back during play times. We enjoyed our break time doing walkovers, flips and handstands up against the wall. I didn't see Catherine again after leaving the home, but we managed to get in touch again in 2002 while I was in London visiting friends. Sadly, since then we have lost touch again.

One of the older boys befriended me too. Richard was the school's kind and caring head boy and was always there to comfort me whenever I suffered with earache – a common occurrence during my infant and junior years. As a result of my earache, I had regular visits to the Bristol ear, Nose and Throat Infirmary and became hard of hearing for a while, something that eventually was corrected. I remember Richard missing his playtime to sit with me next to the heater in the hall while I waited to be taken home due to my awful earache. He showed me a small toy television that displayed cartoon pictures when I turned a button, I was so fascinated with it that he let me keep it.

While we were still in the infants at Top School, my dad turned up one day and took Christine and me out of school, telling the staff he had permission from Auntie Hilda. It was a big surprise for Christine and me. He took us to the place we loved the best in Bristol city centre, Lewis's Store – now a Primark shop. It was a landmark building that stood out because of its great size and curved shape. We had our lunch there at the rooftop restaurant, sitting outside at the tables around a lovely fountain. During our lunch, my dad made us laugh by accidently pouring sugar on his dinner instead of salt. When we'd finished eating, he took us shopping and bought us both a new coat, then took us back to Severnleigh as our time with him was coming an end.

On Lewis's roof with my dad

When the Bertram Mills Circus came to the Downs, the kids from it attended our school. Apart from knowing who they were and saying hello I didn't have much to do with them as I didn't have an outside life after school hours. They were usually only there for a few weeks, but it seemed like months.

'You lot are allowed a treat at the weekend', Auntie Hilda would tell us over breakfast, 'we are all going to the circus, unless you are naughty'. Needless to say we were all on our best behaviour so we could go. As usual, we went to it and thoroughly enjoyed it.

My teachers in the junior school were nice enough, but they each had their nicknames or sayings, and I can remember quite a few of them. Mr Jones – 'You dare move from me boy and I'll wallop you.' Mrs Tazewell – *Tazbag* as she was affectionately known. Mrs Tazewell's sister also taught us, but I can't remember her name! Mr Amesbury was my class teacher and we thought he resembled one of the Marx Brothers with his curled up moustache.

He quite often sent me to stand outside the classroom for talking, nothing has changed there then! When one of the boys swore in class once Mr Amesbury washed his mouth with soap and slapped the palms of his hands with a ruler. Can you imagine lawyers getting their teeth into a teacher if he or she did that these days? It is what was called *discipline*.

Mrs Wheatcroft was of average height, white-haired lady of advanced years and she would often throw her blackboard rubber at my friend, Catherine, for holding hands with a boy named Shane while swinging backwards on their chairs. Mrs Noble persuaded me to play the recorder - not that I needed much encouragement. Miss Coombes wore baggy knee-length bloomers, which she unwittingly displayed to the class by sitting with her legs wide open. Miss Cook was a sweet, 'mummsy' type who taught the first year pupils, while Mr Miles taught the less academic children – known as *special needs* these days. Finally, there was Mrs Davies, the chief dinner lady, who would traipse us around to the dinner halls off Highland Place for lunch.

All through our infant and junior school years, we Muller kids were never allowed to walk to or from school on our own. Instead we all had to wait at the top of Blackboy Hill for one of the aunties to meet us. Our safety was the aunties' sole priority. The walks along Stoke Road to school were fun; we loved to mimic power walkers striding past us at top speed, their bums wiggling from side to side. We'd skip, play hopscotch in the squares on the pavement, sing like the Von Trapp family in *The Sound of Music* and laugh with whichever auntie was escorting us. The Downs were on our right hand side and in the summer they rippled with green grass and gorgeous trees, dotted everywhere. In the winter, the Downs would be covered in crisp white snow after a good fall of it. It would be so very cold walking to school on a morning. Sometimes, the snow was so deep on the Downs that it went over the top and into my welly boots, but that was all part of the fun. Winters were real winters and the summers were real sunny summers. My favourite season was and still is the summer and didn't I just love walking to school wearing our summer clothes.

On route to school, we passed various things that are still there from a long time ago. On the left, side was a huge, ornate, marble drinking-water fountain that had been there since the 1800s, on it the words inscribed - to George W Edwards Esquire, Mayor 1877. Further down the road, nearer school was a very tall, white water tower. I learned years later from Manfred, an ex-Muller man that some of the boys from Alveston Lodge Boys' Home where he had lived, would hide behind this tower while nicking off school! I met Manfred again through another ex-Muller man named Sinjun, who is now living in Australia. Manfred and I met up in Abu Dhabi a few years back and have remained friends. I encouraged him to get his records from the administration office in Bristol where I had received mine, which he did. On the right on the Downs, was an old, battered wooden bus shelter that repeatedly took a hammering whenever the Mods and Rockers had a fracas, it was forever having to be repaired.

In 1963, after doing well in junior school, Christine was placed in Bedminster Down Grammar School. This is when she inherited the nickname of 'Brain Box Willy Warrior', that was a compliment coming from Auntie Hilda, but I'm not sure Christine was that impressed, although she does laugh about it now.

Me, on the other hand did not like school at all, unless it was a subject I enjoyed, needlework, music and P.E, but as it says in my reports – wastes time talking! I always was a chatterbox.

BRISTOL EDUCATION COMMITTEE

ST. JOHN'S J.M. AND INFANTS' SCHOOL

DURDHAM DOWN, BRISTOL, 8

School Report

Name *Linda Warrior*

Class *Junior H.*

129 Edu/20 P&S

Date of Report

3 eb. 1966.

English	Often good work is produced.
Mathematics	Very sound progress has been made but mental work is very difficult for her.
General subjects History Geography Science	Quite sound.
Arts & Crafts Needlework	Good. Very good but wastes time talking
Physical Education & Games	Very good.
Music	Very good. Linda is very keen but must learn to give me all her attention all of the time. AN.

GENERAL REPORT

Linda is capable of quite good work, but quite often she just refuses to make any real effort.

B. Amesbury

Class Teacher

Ww Morgan

Head Teacher

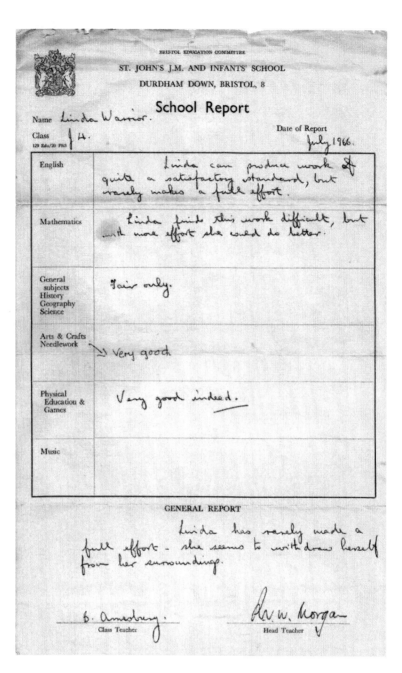

BRISTOL EDUCATION COMMITTEE

ST. JOHN'S J.M. AND INFANTS' SCHOOL

DURDHAM DOWN, BRISTOL, 8

School Report

Name *Linda Warrior.*

Class 4.

129 Edu/20 FN3

Date of Report

July 1966.

English	*Linda can produce work of quite a satisfactory standard, but rarely makes a full effort.*
Mathematics	*Linda finds this work difficult, but with more effort she could do better.*
General subjects History Geography Science	*Fair only.*
Arts & Crafts Needlework	*Very good*
Physical Education & Games	*Very good indeed.*
Music	

GENERAL REPORT

Linda has rarely made a full effort - she seems to withdraw herself from her surroundings.

B. Amesbury.
Class Teacher

W. Morgan
Head Teacher

My last school reports from 1966

114

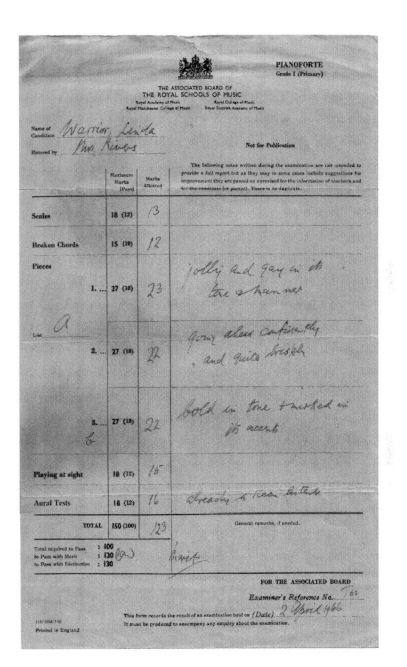

My Piano Exam Certificate, I passed with a merit.

Chapter 14

THE MOVE BACK

Following the summer in 1960, my mother decided to move back to Yorkshire. After renting one room for a while, she found a small house in William Street in Redcar. On 28 September, my mother wrote to Auntie Hilda.

Dear Miss Ashton,
Sorry to have taken so long in writing but I was waiting until I knew my definite address. I have moved out of the one room I had, I dislike eating, cooking and sleeping all in the same room, and it was costing me three pounds and ten shillings just for one room. Now I have taken this small furnished house, it is three pounds 15/- but worth the extra 5/- to have a proper little house of my own. It is very lonely though without the children, I have my neighbour's little girl running in and out like she belonged to me. Still, one day my dreams and prayers will be answered and I will have my own darlings with me for always.
I have not seen anything of my husband since we came back from Bristol, so what he has in mind I don't know? I can't seem to get him to talk things out; he seems so very quiet and distant, still you said it may work out yet. I think perhaps the seaman's strike is worrying him at the moment.
My father is a lot better lately and getting out quite a bit with my brother who is a salesman and also a tailor, He is going to make the girls each a coat, to do this he requires their measurements. If I send you details of how he wants their size perhaps you could fill in the required size etc.; he is a funny one, everything must be done right. He made my oldest brother's 11 year old boy his Grammar School outfit and just because one stitch was wrong on his blazer collar he took the whole collar out and did it again, no one even noticed it but him.
I don't think there is any more news at the moment, oh, just one thing I forgot, my youngest brother still receives the Annual Report and I have been reading and came across a few pictures of Christine and Linda. I was thrilled to pieces when I saw them, especially the one of Linda 'Dreaming' I think it is a delightful

photograph, I can never get her to look so charming. Well I must
close now so hoping to hear from you soon.
God Bless you always,
Very sincerely yours
Phyllis N Norris

Dreaming

Christmas time in Severnleigh

At Christmas, the stair banister was decorated in cotton wool from the top to bottom, with ornamental Santas and his reindeers, snowmen and other Christmas items placed all the way down, which stopped us sliding down it for a while! The windowsill below the stained glass window was also decorated with cotton wool and a Nativity display. It looked so beautiful and Christmassy.

On Christmas morning, after finishing preparing the breakfast, everyone congregated at the top of the stairs ready to sing to Jesus. We were waiting for Auntie Hilda to arrive when Shawn, in his excitement, jumped up at one of the older girls, accidently catching her just under her nose with his paw making her nose bleed. Everything had to be delayed while she was attended to and it wasn't long before we were all lined up and ready to sing. We sang *Happy Birthday* to the huge picture of Jesus that was hung up on the wall then all hurried as sedately as possible to the playroom. I ran down the stairs one year, and got clipped round the ear and made to go back to say sorry to Jesus for being greedy! We opened the playroom door to an awesome sight. Hanging from the big extended fireguard was a long, thick stocking for each one of us with our name on, filled to the brim with toys and games. There was always an apple and an orange along with monkey nuts in it. Underneath each stocking was a box crammed to the top with more presents for each of us. Not one child did without, and the house was buzzing with laughter and excitement. Even Shawn got a new collar, a big bone and chocolate doggy drops.

After we'd finished opening all the presents, we went through into the dining room for breakfast. Auntie Hilda would always say *Grace* before meals to thank the Lord for the food we had been given each day and when we'd finished eating, we'd have a short bible reading. After clearing up the breakfast things, everyone was called into the sitting-room where a couple of aunties had dragged more boxes filled to capacity with presents to be shared out between everybody.

Once we'd opened all the presents and put them away, it was time for church. We'd put on our Sunday best clothes and go to Alma Road Church for morning service. Lots of kids from the other Muller's houses would be there too, it was always nice to see them. After church, we'd go home for our Christmas dinner with all the trimmings you would expect on Christmas day. Dinner was always followed with Christmas pudding and white sauce. I never liked the taste of Christmas pudding but had to eat it anyway. One lucky person would find a sixpence in their pudding, but it was never me. After doing the washing up and having our usual hour's nap, we were given more presents in the staff sitting room. We'd be allowed to play with our new toys for a while, before storing them in our cupboards in the playroom. Before we knew it, it would be tea-time with turkey sandwiches and jelly and ice cream for dessert. Finally people from the Theological College would join us for tea and to sing Christmas carols round the piano, filling the house with music before we went to bed.

I was going to be six on my birthday in February, and was able to understand and appreciate Christmas at Severnleigh a lot more than I had in previous years. We were all looked after so well and there were a lot of kind and generous people who donated presents for our homes. The generosity and care was astonishing, to say the least.

On Boxing Day, we would receive yet more presents. Later in the day, there would be one of Uncle Bob's organised parties for us to attend, where we would meet up with children from some of the other Muller's Homes. We loved being able to dress up in our best clothes to go to these parties.

In 1963 Auntie June announced she would be getting married to Uncle John from the Theological College down the road, they decided to choose Christine and me to be bridesmaids. We were so excited. We had pink velvet dresses made with white velvet edging on the sleeves and matching white velvet headbands, new white shoes and socks. We both felt like princesses for the day. We had lots of fittings until the dresses were perfect, then the big day finally arrived. What a glorious sunny day it was, all the kids and aunties were so excited to be going to the wedding and Christine and I felt privileged to have been asked out of all the kids at Severnleigh to be chosen as bridesmaids. Everyone made their way to Bethesda church in their best clothes ready and waiting patiently for Auntie June, Christine and me to arrive. There were gasps along with a few tears of joy when people saw how beautiful Auntie June looked on entering the church. We also could hear people commenting how lovely Christine and I looked and a few comments were made on how cute we were too. Uncle John, his best man and his friends all wore top hat and tails and looked very dashing. After the ceremony, the reception was held at Severnleigh. There were a lot of photographs taken in the gardens on this special day - a day that I will never forget.

Bridesmaids feeling special

We were allowed to wear the dresses to the next Boxing Day party and felt so special and pretty. Eventually, we outgrew the dresses and they were handed down to someone else.

Auntie June and Uncle John's Wedding

Auntie June and Uncle John with me in 2002

Chapter 15
OFF TO SEA

Late in 1960, mother applied to join the Merchant Navy. She had met a man, who was living in South Africa and the only way she could get to see him again, was to travel. Sailing around the world wasn't a bad way to earn a living. In the meantime, while waiting for a reply from the Merchant Navy, she wrote to Muller's asking if she could have us home for a time during the summer holidays.

The reply from Mrs Horne, 9 February, 1961:

Dear Mrs Norris
Miss Ashton has sent on to me your letter suggesting that you might be able to have the two girls for a time during their summer holiday. This would be alright if you could fetch them and bring them back yourself.
Will you be able to afford this long journey to and fro twice? Also it would be alright if you are taking them to your father's house. We should be quite pleased for them to visit him.
Perhaps you will be able to come down and visit the children before the summer holidays and will come and have a talk with me about the possibilities of this visit.
In the meantime it will be wise to say nothing at all to the girls about it in case it does not come to anything.
Yours sincerely
Mrs Horne

My mother was granted permission to have us home to Redcar for two weeks in the summer of 1961.

We stayed with her at Grandad Smith's in Cleveland Street, near the main Post Office. We had such a lovely time meeting mother's friends and members of our family we didn't even know we had. On a few occasions, our Auntie Cynthia, who was mother's cousin, took us both to the beach for the day where we had donkey rides and ice cream. She was kind to us and she always made time for Christine and me. She and my mother spent a lot of time together - they were more like best friends than cousins. Auntie Cynthia was an attractive, smartly-dressed, feisty lady and a hard worker. A few years later, we lost touch when she went to live in South Africa in 1962 with her husband. She was a devoted wife to her late husband, Don. Last I heard was that she is still living there but, sadly, not in very good health.

Auntie Cynthia with Granddad Smith

Granddad Smith with Christine and me in Albert Park

Although Granddad couldn't cope with us living with him when we were little, it wasn't because he didn't love us. It was because he was not in good enough health to be able cope with two babies. He was a quite a small man with a good heart, he was kind and gentle and I cared about him so much. We loved spending time with him. During our holiday, he would sometimes take us with him to Albert Park in Middlesbrough, where he drove a mini steam train during the day-time We were allowed to stay on it for as long as we wanted; we must have gone round twenty times or more, and had hours of fun on that train with him. The other kids didn't get a look in when it came to sitting at the front. We let them know in no uncertain terms that he was *our* Grandad, so they would have to sit at the back. When the day drew to a close he took us back to Redcar on the bus, when we arrived home we would be bursting with excitement to tell our mother over tea, what a great day we'd had.

One day my mother took us for a day out to meet friends of hers in Middlesbrough, some of our Warrior relatives lived there too, so this was an opportunity to meet them again as I was a baby last time I saw them. Christine and I spent most of the day playing outside in the street with them, getting to know each other and loving the freedom while the adults sat chatting over cups of tea. That day was such good fun and after that we went back on quite a few more occasions. Eventually we lost touch.

The Warriors

My Grandad Smith had moved from Middlesbrough and was now living in Redcar in a small terraced house in Cleveland Street. On the left side of his house was an alleyway that led to a gate and back yard that housed an outside toilet, the alley had an uneven cobble-stoned pathway that echoed if I was shouting for Christine to come and play with me. We played twosey-ball on the wall, driving Grandad mad at times with the banging and echoing! Next door but was a quaint sweet shop owned by a lovely old lady. Its shelves were always stacked to the brim with large jars of sweets. I would often disappear after my bath wearing just my pyjamas; my mother knew she would find me in there, spending my pennies that Grandad had given to me. Next door but one to the sweet shop was the town's main post office. The promenade and beach was only a short walk away, just a couple of hundred yards or so, Christine would hold my hand all the way to the beach, passing the little shop where buckets and spades and beach balls were hung outside for sale. We had hours of fun looking for crabs, starfish and anything else we could find to take home in our buckets. As Christine was two years my elder, she was allowed to take me and never let me out of her sight, but you could guarantee I would came home soaking wet every time!

'The waves came up and hit me, mummy!' I said innocently. I suppose that's what I felt had happened.

One day, on the way home from the beach with Christine, I was eager to get back to show Grandad my collection of shells and crabs, that I pulled away from Christine dashing into the road in front of an oncoming car. Thankfully I wasn't injured, just a bit shaken. The driver who had bumped me was also shaken, but, he and his wife made sure that I was alright and comforted me before taking me home. All the same, I learned my lesson and didn't run away from Christine into the road again.

My mother always dressed very smartly and looked elegant, keeping her hair immaculate at all times. One day as she was going to her regular hairdresser in the town, she took us with her to have our hair curled. It felt great as we were never allowed to have any hairstyle other than the 'basin' cut in the home. Looking at the photos now we looked a bit stupid, but as kids we felt so grown up, loving it.

At the end of our holiday we had to go back to Severnleigh. It was hard parting with my family, but that's the way it had to be. My mother had signed papers stating that we would be in Muller's Homes until we were fifteen years of age, or until such time as she could find a decent job and provide a stable home for us. My mother was still trying to get into the Merchant Navy, but she wasn't having much luck. However, her luck was about to change.

Christmas arrived and with it, all the good times as usual. We helped with the decorations as always, we even had chocolate money bags hanging from the tree to be shared out as an extra-special treat. After Christmas, we all went back to school, and the aunties stayed at home, caring for the house and carrying on with the normal everyday routine.

My mother wrote to Auntie Hilda on 26 January, 1962

My dear Miss. Aston,
Just a line hoping you are well. I am not too bad but have had four days in bed. It's a carry on, these colds. Still I must admit I feel better after my rest. It must pay to stay in bed.
Have you heard any more from Mr Norris? I have written to him twice to ask him to call and see me, but he has ignored my letters, I do want to get things sorted out. He told my mother he was courting and immigrating to New Zealand. If he does that without first giving me my freedom he can't think much of the girls and my happiness. If I had been free, both the girls and probably my father if he had been in the best of health- would have gone to live in Canada by now. My father's brother and his family are forever asking us to go out there. They have their own business have come along fine.
Just think if I had been free to go and prepare a home for the girls, it would have given them a new life completely in a new country. Still that's the way of fate.
I keep on praying that my husband will think of my happiness for a change.
It seems that all our family are immigrating. I have now got four or five uncles in USA and my cousin and her family went a few months ago. All are doing very well and now my cousin Cynthia and her husband are going to California this year. Maybe something will turn up so I can go with my family.

Meanwhile I have got to get rid of my cold first and foremost or I won't be going anywhere.
I do hope you are personally keeping well, I know it must take it out of you at times having the worries of the small children. I perhaps shouldn't burden you with all my personal problems, but I feel so much better for having you to tell. I can't talk to anyone up here, they don't understand of my strong feeling of wanting to do the best for my girls.
Well, I won't keep you with my problems any longer so until next time cheerio for now and God Bless you always.
Yours very sincerely
Mrs N Norris

My seventh birthday was on 26 February, 1962, and mother received a letter from the Merchant Navy saying she had been accepted as a stewardess. She would be sailing on 7 March, 1962, her job would involve singing, entertaining and looking after the children on board. My mother didn't manage to get another visit to see us before she set sail. However, she did send us amazing postcards that we looked forward to receiving, from every port she visited. They were always fancy, unusual cards with embroidered dancers or bull fighters so we knew which countries she had been to. Although she sent us cards from all around the world, she never did manage to send a card from South Africa. I know from her letters that she had particularly wanted to go there to see a man that she had cared for, but I can only assume she never managed to do this.

On 3 April, 1962, my mother had been at sea for one month. She wrote this letter from Cunard Steam Ship Co Ltd, R.M.S. SYLVANIA, LIVERPOOL, 3, addressed to Muller's:
Dear Mrs Horne,
Just a line to enclose the form back, also two pounds towards the girl's upkeep, It is not a lot at the moment but I expect to be able to send you more at a future date. I am settling down nicely in my new job, though it is long hours and we are kept busy, but I think it will be worthwhile in the long run.

I do hope you are all keeping well and trust the girls are too. I thank you very sincerely for all your kindness towards my little girls.
Very sincerely yours
Mrs N Norris

Mother stayed in the Merchant Navy for over two years until November 1964, travelling around the world. We didn't see much of her during those two years, but she would telephone when she could every-time her ship was in dock. On her few returns to the UK, she would try and visit us at Severnleigh. She always brought a gift for us both from at least one of the different countries she had visited on her travels. When she could, she would also bring gifts for the aunties and one time Auntie June received a pair of cream silk pyjamas. On my mother's visits, if she could get to Bristol early enough, she would take us shopping in the morning to buy us new clothes. We wore our new clothes proudly, usually to church on a Sunday or if we were going out for tea. She liked us to look like the sisters we were and tried to get us both the same style dress but different colours, we loved the fact that the clothes were new and not hand-me-downs. I especially loved my blue dress with a big white bow on the front. Christine had the same dress in orange. We wore them on a day out to Portishead with my mother and her best friend, Auntie Joan from London. Auntie Joan was a fun person to be with: very tall and elegant in her high heeled shoes and fine clothes. She was always immaculately dressed. I don't think I ever saw her without wearing lipstick and make-up. My mother and Joan were thick as thieves and made a lot of memories with each other.

Day out at Portishead with Auntie Joan and my mother

My dad was also still in the Merchant Navy. He would come to see us occasionally when on leave. On one of Dad's visits, he brought two of the tallest dolls I'd ever seen for Christine and me - they were even taller than me! On another occasion, he brought us two-tone purple and pink grass skirts and yellow and blue garland necklaces from Hawaii, or some such exotic country. We had great fun dressing up in them in the play-room

Chapter 16

MY FRIEND JONTY and my RETURN TO MULLER'S

It was during my time in the infants' school that Jonathan (Jonty) and I first befriended each other. We were never far away from each other in school. In junior school we couldn't wait for break time so we could play bulldog under the Arches. Jonty often helped me whenever I got stuck with my school work and always encouraged me to do better. He remained my best friend all through our infant and junior years. Jonty had two brothers, Simon, who was older than him and Nick, he was the youngest. They had the best parents anyone could wish for. They were such kind and caring people. Jonty's dad, Brian, worked for the BBC in Bristol. His mum was a stunning lady with dark hair, cut in a 1960's style bob, which she often wore with a silk scarf round it and long ties at the back.

On some Saturdays, Jonty's parents would invite me to their house in Arlington Villas for tea which they always made special with sandwiches and cakes, ice cream and jelly. I loved going to their house and went whenever I was invited. Early on one Saturday evening, they took me back to Severnleigh after spending the day with them. It was a lovely, warm summer's day and while Jonty's mum and dad were chatting with Auntie Hilda, Jonty and I were playing by rolling down the hill where the memorial cross was situated. The fun came to an abrupt end though when Jonty rolled awkwardly and broke his arm. After a trip to the hospital, Jonty's arm was put in a plaster cast for a few weeks. We played with caution on that hill after that.

Jonty and I remained friends until I left the orphanage in 1966 to live with my mother in Yorkshire. I did see him when Christine and I returned to Severnleigh for a holiday the following year and again four years later on a flying visit to Bristol, but sadly that was the last time I ever saw my friend Jonty.

In 2002, a new website called *Friends Reunited* appeared on the internet. I decided I would try and find some of the children from the Muller's orphanage. My efforts proved fruitless. Of course, I also looked up my friend Jonty, but couldn't find him either. I did, however, find Nick, his younger brother and to make sure it was really him, I wrote to Nick giving the names of Jonty's parents and the address at which they'd lived. To my delight Nick emailed back telling me he was indeed the right person and asked my connection with Jonty. I explained everything about our friendship at school and the visits I had had to his house for tea on Saturdays. I knew that Nick and Simon had gone to the same school as Jonty and me and that Simon was the same age as Christine and Nick was the youngest. Finally, I explained that I was trying to locate Jonty to see how he was doing.

Nick replied with a very sad message: Jonty had passed away in the year 2000.

I was stunned and devastated. I struggled to contain my tears. Why was I feeling so sad? After all, we hadn't been in touch for years; not since 1971, in fact. Why did I feel this way? I felt there was a reason for this and wanted to know more about what happened in Jonty's life since leaving school. I wanted to know more about my life living in Bristol too. I had recently been contemplating re-searching my past in Bristol and discovering that Jonty had passed away made me all the more determined not to lose any more time. This determination led me back to the orphanage to find my records and I set off on a mission to re-search my childhood that I had spent in the George Muller orphanage.

I stayed in touch with Nick and through him, made contact with his mum. I told Jonty's mum I was going to fly over to the UK (I am living in the Middle East at this time in my life) then drive to Bristol, I asked would she mind if I came to see her. She replied that she would be happy for me to come to her home. I was delighted. I made all the arrangements and flew over with my youngest son Robert and we stayed in a hotel in Bristol.

Jonty's mum arranged for Simon to be there for mine and Roberts visit, but unfortunately Nick had other commitments so I didn't get to see him. She made us a lovely cottage pie dinner and over a glass of wine showed me lots of photos of Jonty growing up. It was surreal. She told me of the sad time when Jonty became ill and the sad story of when he passed away, she told me also that her husband, Brian, had also passed away twenty years before. This was such a shame as I would have loved to have seen them again; I had just left it too late and wished I had looked them up years earlier. I will never forget that family and the kindness they showed to me as a child.

During the two weeks I spent in Bristol, I took a trip to the Muller House administration office in Cotham Park, to collect my records from all those years ago. The records consisted of the correspondence between my mother and the Muller Homes and had been kept for me all those years. Wendy, Julian and other members of staff that worked there gave me a warm welcome. I followed Wendy into a private room where I sat down at a huge old brown table with bulbous legs, just like the ones we'd used in our dining room back in Severnleigh. The room was adorned with tall glass fronted book cases that were filled with row upon row of books about George Muller's life and work. A beautiful picture of George Muller had a prime place up on the wall above an old fashioned fireplace. I waited patiently until Wendy brought my records to me. Filled with nervousness and excitement at what I was about to read, I took a deep breath and proceeded to read the letters that had been written between my mother and the Muller staff over the previous years. I struggled to take it all in at that moment and was feeling a bit uncomfortable reading them in front of someone else. It was also taking up far too much of my time as I wanted to look around the house and the museum, so decided to leave the rest until later when I could read and absorb them in private.

Putting the letters aside, I asked Wendy if I could have a look around the Muller House administration building as I had known it as a child. She took me into the garden. Immediately, I saw the large conservatory attached to the back of the house that had been there for years. It had been refurbished and inside, had been converted into an exotic garden with soft, calming, waterfalls and flowers. I remembered having seen it as a child and thinking it looked so much more modern compared to the rest of the house. I wandered around the garden, which was as I had remembered it: green lawns surrounded by tall trees from the days when Muller's would hold a garden tea party for the homes. My son, Robert and I, took turns pushing each other on the swing that I had played on as a child during my visits. It was still hanging from the same enormous old tree with thick twisted rope, although I'm sure the rope had been renewed a few times since then. Precious memories were flooding back from my childhood days spent Muller's. The tour around the garden was magical and a little emotional, but I also felt overjoyed to be there. I would have loved to been able to stay there longer as I enjoyed it so much but I had to press on with other plans I had made for that day.

After my tour around the garden, Wendy took me to a room that had been converted into a small Museum, with memorabilia dating back to the 1800s when the late, great George Muller had begun to build his orphanages. The amount of memorabilia in such a small room was remarkable. George Muller's original desk was there, it is over 200 years old. There was a dolls' house that had been constructed to look identical to the main houses on Ashley Down. Album after album of photographs contained pictures dating from the very first Muller's orphans to the very last, plus there was a photo section in a glass cabinet on the wall titled 'Muller's Weddings'. Among the wedding photos was a picture of Christine and me when we were bridesmaids for Auntie June and Uncle John in 1963. There is too much memorabilia in the museum to mention everything, but if you wish to visit, it is open to the public during office hours. And I have to say, well worth a visit.

After spending a few hours there, the time came when I had to leave and said my goodbyes to Wendy, Julian and all the lovely staff at Muller House Administration Office who had been kind enough to help with my research. Robert and I then headed off to Ashley Down to see the first orphanage I had stayed in. It was poignant going back inside this mammoth building, knowing I had lived there at one point in my life and more-so, being part of the history even though I had been too young to remember anything about that time, unfortunately.

I drove over to the Downs to Stoke Bishop with Robert to show him Severnleigh, the place where I had spent over nine years of my youth. I stood in awe, looking at the house and remembering every part of it. From the outside, I described it room by room to him and recalled my experiences with fondness. The plaque on wall to the entrance of the house is still embellished with the title name of 'Severnleigh' and while I was admiring it, a lady entered the driveway and I began chatting with her, she told me the building was apartments and asked if I was looking for one. I then told her that a long time ago, the building had been one of George Muller orphanages for quite a number of years, also that I had lived there for the best part of nine years. This came as a complete surprise to her. To my delight, she asked if I would like to come inside - she didn't need to ask me twice!

As soon as I entered through that familiar, big, old front door, I felt a mixture of feelings I can't explain. It was magical: nervousness, with a rush of excitement and happiness all together. I looked to my left to where the kitchen had been, and it was now an entrance to someone's flat. Ahead of me, where the dining room, living room and playroom had been, all I could see were entrance doors to the rooms that were now apartments. All the rooms had been converted into self-contained flats. As I looked left to the staircase, to my surprise II noticed that the old thick brown banister and the original stained glass window were still there and seeing them took me right back to standing on the stairs singing to Jesus on Christmas morning - and all the times I'd slid down that banister! It was an amazing feeling. I went up the six or so stairs to the landing, there again there were just doors leading to apartments, but I was very happy the lady had allowed me to go in and see the lovely place in which I had spent my childhood.

I returned back to see Severnleigh in 2010 with my surrogate sister, Jayne, I wanted to show her the beautiful house I had been brought up in. While we were in the back garden picking up pine cones and admiring the building, a man appeared from what used to be the basement to find out why we were there. When I told him a little of the history, he asked if we would like to come into his flat for a look around. Once again I was ecstatic to do so. His flat was beautifully furnished, bright and modern, but still had some of the original pipes and fittings. I described to him what each room had been used for and what had been in them all those years ago. The man was amazed; he'd had no idea he was living in what had been one of the famous George Muller orphanages. Over a cup of tea, I told him and his wife all about it, they both hung on to my every word. He was very grateful to me and told me he was so intrigued that he would look up more information on the history of the Muller Homes. After having a wonderful time there, it was finally time for us to move on, we reluctantly wished the people well and said our goodbyes.

Chapter 17

A NEW HOME

During the summer of 1964 all the children from Severnleigh and various other Muller Homes were taken on a camping holiday to the Isle-of-Wight. While there, we were joined by a hundred or so people from Merthyr Tydfil in Wales, with whom we had previously stayed for a weekend. Lots and lots of tents were put up for us all to sleep in and one enormous marquee was erected to be used for dining, church services singing and bible readings. The Welsh people are renowned for their amazing choir voices; it was glorious to hear the beautiful sound of singing echoing around the marquee and campsite.

Camping Holiday in the Isle-of-White

During our holiday there, we had lovely evening walks with the aunties and to see the 'Needles' lighthouse where we bought multi-coloured sand in lighthouse shaped glass bottles. We went to the beach and played with the animals on the nearby farm. The Muller's staff organised games on the campsite for us and the children from Wales. Unfortunately, I got sick for a while. Auntie Hilda took me to a doctor's which seemed like a ten mile hike away from the campsite, but at least I was given medication and recovered enough to enjoy the rest of my holiday

On 18 November, 1964, my mother wrote to Mrs Horne.

Dear Mrs Horne,
Just a line to let you know I have decided to settle at home with
my mother. I have a job as a waitress in a hotel and we have
discussed the possibility of having Christine and Linda back home.
We are moving into our new house in two weeks' time which is
large enough for us all and we have a large garden and fairly
close to the newly built schools. Would you be kind enough to let
me know your views as I would very much like to have the girl's
home, I would much rather have seen you to talk over this, but at
the moment it is impossible for me to take time off work.
A further matter, I have only just found out that Mr Warrior has not
been paying in Christine's one pound a week, would you please
let me know if you can when the last payment from Middlesbrough
Town Clerks Office. I should be very grateful and pleased to hear
from you. Trusting you are in good health.
God's blessing on you.
Yours sincerely
Phyllis N Norris

On 25 November, 1964, Muller's wrote:

Dear Mrs Norris,
I was very surprised to have your letter and learn that you have
left the people you were with, which you thought was an excellent
opening for you. I do hope that you will settle down happily with
your mother and find being with her gives you the help and
support you need.
In view of the fact that you have changed around so often in these
last years, I do very strongly advise you to wait awhile and make
quite sure that this present arrangement is really going to last
before you attempt to have the children back to live with you. I
know that is what you want and they want it too, but we are very
concerned at the unsettling effect your many changes have had
on them and should be sorry if you had them hastily and then the
arrangement broke down. I shall be very glad too if you do not say
anything to them which will make them think they will be coming to

you permanently until you and you mother are both quite sure how this is going to work out.
When you are next able to come down and see them I shall be glad of the opportunity to have a talk with you again. It is very good in spite of all your changes you have managed to keep in touch regularly with the children so they have no fear of your having forgotten them.
The last payment made from Middlesbrough Magistrates' Clerk's Office was on 21st February 1958. The only amounts received since then have been those from you.
With all good wishes
Yours sincerely
Muller's

Christine's dad hadn't paid anything towards her keep for nearly seven years and my dad simply didn't pay at all. The following year, we were allowed to go home to Redcar for the summer holidays again. We couldn't wait!

On 29 June, 1965, Muller's wrote:

Dear Mrs Norris,
I understand that you are coming to fetch the girls for their holiday on Saturday July 24thand I shall be very glad if you will arrange to come up here first so that we may have a short talk. I shall be glad of the opportunity of seeing you.
With all good wishes
Yours sincerely
Muller'

My mother came for us on 24 July, as promised and took us home to Redcar for our five weeks' summer holiday. We were so excited about going home and staying with mother at Nana Smith's house in Ambleside Avenue. Christine had her thirteenth birthday on 27 July, and mother took us to Vogue hairdressers in Queen Street, to have our hair curled while Nana made cakes and jelly for the birthday party that afternoon. Christine dressed in her favourite orange dress with a long white bow and me in my blue one. Then all our new friends arrived for Christine's birthday party.

138

Christine's Thirteenth birthday

Our holiday was saddened during the first week due to our Grandad Smith passing away on 29 July. It was a really sad time for us all as we all cared so much for him, but mother still did the best she could to give us a good holiday. Christine and I had a great time going to the seaside, the parks and the shops, along with meeting new friends. Often my mother would take us to the Merchant Navy Hotel in Middlesbrough, where she knew a lot of people from her time working at sea.

The staff that worked there treated us kindly and spoilt us both by providing us with crisps and fizzy drinks. (All the healthy stuff) 'What sweet girls they are' people would say, and 'How well-mannered they are'. Our summer holiday seemed to go on for such a long time and we both loved every minute of it, but eventually, the day in August came when we had to go back to Severnleigh.

At the Merchant Navy Hotel in Middlesbrough

On 11 August, 1965, my mother wrote to Muller's:

Dear Mrs Horne,
Just a line to let you know the girls will be returning on the 28th
August. I would so much like to have kept them home but my
mother feels it would be too much for her at the moment as she is
suffering so much lately with rheumatism. I really am disappointed
of course as I was looking forward to keeping the girls home this
time. Perhaps I can do something by Christmas about having my
own place. I shall certainly do my utmost. Having the girl's home
this past two weeks has made a big difference to me and I shall
miss them terribly when I bring them back again. They have had a
lovely time and been such a comfort to me since my father passed
away two weeks ago.
We have not had much good weather at all, but enjoyed ourselves
just the same. I shall not be able to call on you this time as I shall
have to be on my way back to Redcar as early as possible, but I
shall certainly see you in a couple of months' time. My best wishes
to you.
God bless you
Sincerely yours

Phyllis N Norris.

On 16 August, 1965, Muller's wrote:
Dear Mrs Norris,
Thank you very much for your letter and I was very sorry indeed to hear of the death of your father. I would like to send very sincere sympathy to your mother and yourself. I do hope that having the little girls with you was a comfort and a help.
They will be expected back at 'Severnleigh' on the 29th August and I do hope it will not be very long after that before you are able to make the permanent arrangements for them to stay at home with you.
With all good wishes
Yours sincerely
Mrs Horne.

Back at school, I was struggling to concentrate as all I could think about was my wonderful holiday, the lovely time Christine and I had had with my mother in Redcar and all my new friends there. I hadn't wanted it to end; none of us did.

On 9 November, 1965, my mother wrote to Muller's:

Dear Mrs Horne,
Just a line to let you know my divorce case is finally to be heard on the 19th of this month.
I am not sure but I think my solicitor will be writing to you to verify whether or not I have kept in touch with the children regularly or just deposited them in your care and forgot about them, I must say I was surprised when he asked me such a question, as he knows the girls have always been first and foremost in my mind. He has explained the judge of the case will want proof. I realize of course that it is necessary to have your verification. I shall be very pleased and relieved to have it all over and done with, then I can start my life afresh and plan our futures. I do so long to have the girls home for good, even my mother misses them terribly now, after having them around her for a few weeks.

141

Do you know if Linda is up to grammar school education?
Because if she is it would be a shame to interrupt her education
before she got into grammar school. If I bring them now or within
the next three to four months she would have to sit the eleven plus
exam here. Perhaps you would be kind as to let me know your
views. I must close now, but I hope you did not mind my writing to
you to let you know what is happening, trusting you are keeping
well.
God bless you always
Phyllis N Norris.

On 9 November, 1965, my mother's solicitor did indeed write
to Muller's.

Dear Mrs Horne,
We act for Mrs Phyllis Noreen Norris of Ambleside Ave, Redcar in
connection with her divorce case which is due to be heard at
Stockton on the 19th November 1965.
In her divorce petition she is claiming custody of Christine and
Linda whom we know are living in the home.
We have known Mrs Norris for some time and she has always
seemed to us to be concerned about the welfare of her children.
We would like to produce to the court if possible a letter from you
indicating that she has shown interest in her children and that she
has regularly corresponded with them and been in contact with
them since they were first put in your care. We would be very
grateful if you could kindly write to us and confirm these matters
and add anything else which you think is important with regard to
the children and their mother. We have in mind that the children
are now settled at the Home but that Mrs Norris would like to bring
them home to Redcar as soon as she is able to find suitable
accommodation.
Your help in the matter would be appreciated.
On a more personal matter the writer is interested to know to
whom any contribution towards the upkeep of the Home might be
made and would be grateful for any details of the Home's work
which you could send.

Yours truly,
(A solicitor in Redcar)

On 10 November, 1965, Muller's wrote to my mother.
Dear Mrs Norris,
Thank you for your letter letting me know that the divorce is to be heard this month. I have heard from the solicitor about this too. I do most sincerely hope that when this matter is settled you will seriously consider how you can best make for yourself a more settled way of life so as to give to your girls. They do not doubt your love for them but they are becoming very weary of the constant changes in your life and continual discussion of new plans which are soon to be abandoned. Perhaps now, with your mother's backing, you may be able to set up a home and give them what they need from you in the way of good security and a good example.
With regard to Linda's school prospects we think that she will be quite up to the standard of grammar school education if she will work. She will not, however, sit the eleven-plus examination here as they are not holding it anymore in Bristol.
I shall be glad to know the result of the court hearing and how things go with you after that.
Yours sincerely
Mrs Horne.

This letter was written by Muller's for the solicitors to use in court:

10th November 1965.

Christine WARRIOR 27 - 7 - 1952
Linda WARRIOR   26 -2 - 1955
In reply to your enquiry, these children came into the care of these Homes in December 3rd 1957 as their mother was unable to support them and give adequate care. She has moved about a great deal since then but has corresponded regularly, has visited them when she could and has occasionally had them with her for a holiday.

Both children have suffered some disturbance due to their mother's unsettled life and constant changes, and are becoming critical of this. I am sure, however, that they do not doubt her affection for them. They are both intelligent, attractive little girls. Christine is in the Grammar Stream of a Comprehensive School and Linda has a good chance of reaching this. She suffers a slight degree of deafness but this is under specialist treatment and does not seem to have hindered her school work.
If there are any other details you wish to know about, I shall be pleased to answer any questions.
Thank you for the interest expressed in your final paragraph. I enclose a copy of our current report which will give you the information you want.
Yours sincerely
Mrs Horne.

The solicitors' reply to Muller's: On 16 November, 1965

Dear Mrs Horne,
Re: Christine Warrior and Linda Warrior.
We thank you for your letter of the 10th November, received this morning and we are much obliged for your help in the matter. We note what you say in connection with the two children and thank you for enclosing your current report.
Yours sincerely
(A Redcar solicitor)

There was a glimmer of light at the end of the tunnel now my mother was really hoping this was all going to turn out right and then she would be able to bring us home for good. She took this hope with her to court, but unfortunately, her case was adjourned to a later date. The judge wasn't satisfied.

On 24 November, My mother wrote to Muller's.

Dear Mrs Horne,
Just to inform you that my divorce case was adjourned on Friday. The judge was not entirely satisfied with the case so I have to start

all over again. I have to see my solicitor today to go over the case again. I shall keep you informed as to the proceedings. I must admit I was most disappointed at the outcome but god willing everything will turn out right in the end. Trusting you are well and I do thank you for all your help and kindness.
God bless you always.
Sincerely yours
Phyllis N Norris.

Christine and I stayed at Severnleigh for another Christmas, which was as good as all the other years had been, but by this time all we were thinking about was going home to live with our mother. We went into the New Year, going back to school as usual. It was 1966. I was coming up to eleven years of age in February and would be leaving junior school in the summer ready to start at a senior school, but it was still uncertain whether it would be in Bristol or in Redcar. The ideal plan would be to get us home to mother during the summer, so we could start a new school in Redcar after the holiday.

On 15 March, 1966, my mother's solicitors wrote to Mrs Horne.

Dear Mrs Horne,
You kindly wrote to us on the 10th November 1965 about Mrs Norris's children. At the resumed hearing of her divorce certain dates will be important. It would be of considerable assistance to us if you could kindly let us know the dates when Christine and Linda have stayed with their mother since the children came to the Home in 1957. We think particularly that there was an occasion in about the summer of 1961 and if you could let us have these dates from your records we would be very grateful.
As a matter of courtesy we enclose a stamped addressed envelope for your use.
Yours faithfully
(Solicitor in Redcar)

Muller's replied to mother's solicitors on 17 March 1966.

145

Dear Sirs,
Re- Christine and Linda WARRIOR

In reply to your enquiry of March 15th, these children stayed with their mother last year from July 24th to August 27th they also spent a holiday with her in 1961 from July 29th to August 18th.
If they stayed with her any other time I cannot now give you the dates as the records of holiday dates are not kept for such a long time afterwards and I have obtained the 1961 date by looking through a journal for that year.
If there is any question of another stay with her and Mrs. Norris can give the approximate date, I will look this up to verify it, but otherwise could only find it by looking through journals as we still have which would be rather a lengthy business.
I can also confirm that Mrs Norris has kept regularly in touch with the children throughout their time with us by visits and letters or telephone calls.
I hope this covers the information you want. Please let me know if there is anything else you want.
Yours faithfully
Mrs Horne.

Chapter 18

THE LEAVING ARRANGEMENTS

At last things were looking up for my mother. There was a real hope she could get us back home to live with her as she now had a place to live in Ambleside Avenue with our Nana Smith. She had a steady job and for the first time in a long time she was on track. The only thing outstanding was the question of the divorce that hadn't yet been granted.

On 27 April, 1966, my mother wrote to Mrs Horne.

Dear Mrs Horne,
I hope this letter finds you in the best of health.
I am writing to see if I can start to make arrangements for the girls to come home for good in July, when they begin their vacation. Everything is quite in order for them at home, but I was not sure what to do about the school arrangements, perhaps you could inform me as to your wishes etc. I am looking forward to having Linda and Christine home at last for good, trusting to hear from you soon.
God bless you.
Yours sincerely
Phyllis N Norris.

On 29 April, 1966, Muller's replied

Dear Mrs Norris,
Thank you for your letter. We are very glad to know that your affairs are more settled. And hope very much that you will now be able to make a real home for yourself and the children with no more upsets or movements.
We shall be glad to know just what the position is. Did the divorce go through, and what are your plans after that?
Will you be living with your mother or have you a house for yourself and your children and, if so, will there be proper care for them if you are going out to work? You can probably draw

National Assistance so that you only need to do part time, and it is really important that you should make sure of being at home when they come home from school.

You will have to apply to local schools to receive them in September, or you could apply to your Central Education Office to ask where they should be sent. Christine is in the Grammar stream of a Comprehensive School and Linda will be going on to Secondary School next term. She has not taken the eleven plus examination as Bristol has done away with that. I will notify the schools here about their going, and we will have them ready for you on the date you tell us that you can come for them at the end of July.

We shall be reporting their going to your local children's department and you may find it helpful to be able to consult them from time to time. They will certainly not interfere with you in any way, but will take a friendly interest in helping you do the best for your girls.

With all good wishes
Yours sincerely
Mrs Horne.

On 4 May, 1966, my mother wrote to Muller's.

Dear Mrs Horne,
Thank you very much for your letter, I was pleased to hear from you.

The position at the moment of my divorce is that I am just waiting for a re-hearing date which should not be very long now. I intend to devote all my time to the girls. I am not going to re-marry at all, should I get my divorce, and I have quite a good job as an inspector in the factory of the General Electric Company in Middlesbrough. I have been there almost three months now and quite settled. I finish work at 4.15pm and I do not work on Saturday or Sunday. We are making our home with my mother and she will be taking care of the girls on a morning after I have left for work.

I shall more than likely be home before they arrive home from school. In any case my mother will be here as she cooks dinner

for me coming home from work every day. She is looking forward to having the girls to take care of. I shall arrange an appointment to see our Local Education Officer for this coming week end regarding the girl's School's, we have no Comprehensive school here only the Grammar and Secondary, so they will probably attend these respectively. I shall certainly be glad of any help or advice the local children's officer can give me at any time, I shall not think of it as interfering. I will be able to collect my daughters on the 23rd July, if there is anything further you wish to know, I shall be very pleased to hear from you and will inform you regarding the school arrangements etc. thanking you once again for your very kind letter. God bless you.
Very sincerely yours
Phyllis N Norris.

At last something was happening. Muller's wrote to the County Children's Officer in Northallerton. Obviously my mother hadn't brought us up and wasn't sure how to look after us, so she would need some help and guidance on what to do.

On 8 June, 1966

Dear Sir,
Re: Mrs Phyllis N Norris
25 Ambleside Ave Redcar.
Mrs Norris' two children Christine Warrior (27 – 7 – 52) and Linda Warrior (26 – 2 – 55) have been in our care since December 1957 and she now hopes to resume care of them at the end of this school term. We shall be most grateful if a friendly visit can be paid to ensure that she is making suitable arrangements with a reasonable hope of stability. She is a very friendly person, I have told her I would ask for your interest and she is quite happy to expect this.
This was a private placing, on her own application, supported by a Middlesbrough Probation Officer, Miss N M Cooper.
She was then Mrs Warrior, living in lodgings in Middlesbrough, her home town, but was on bad terms with her parents, divorced from her husband, the father of Christine; she had quarrelled with

Linda's father (Norris, to whom she was then not married) and he was not supporting her. She had to go out to work and the children were suffering from lack of proper care – she applied to these homes because her brother had been brought up in them. She married Norris in 1958 but they soon parted again and she is now engaged in divorce proceedings.

Mrs Norris is an affectionate mother and has never failed to keep in touch with her children. She is a most unstable person, and has been in a number of different posts both here and abroad. She has also formed many attachments, which have not lasted and always thinks that the latest plan or friendship is the most desirable thing which will last forever and enable her to make a wonderful home for her children. The children are fond of her still but have become a good deal disillusioned by these changes and unfulfilled promises.

Mrs Norris and her mother – Mrs Smith – now have a house together and the idea is that Mrs Norris can go out to work as granny will be there for the children.

The children went there for part of last summer holidays and we were a good deal concerned at their accounts afterwards of mother's being so frequently out, often very late, and this when they were only there for a fortnight's visit. We shall be very glad indeed to know that some watch will be kept on this family which may also supply a steadying influence on the mother,
Yours sincerely
Mrs Horne.

On 9 June 1966, my mother wrote to Muller's.

Dear Mrs Horne,
Just a line to let you know I have been to the Education Officer in Redcar only to be told we have to get in touch with the Chief Education Officer, County Hall, Northallerton asking him for details regarding Christine and Linda's respective schools. He can only decide which one's I'm told if I can provide him with necessary reports and grading from the girls school in Bristol. I wonder if you would be so kind as to look into this for me. I do so appreciate your help and advice.

I'm told by Miss. Ashton that the girls do not break up from school until the 29th July. I don't suppose it is possible for them to leave a little sooner is it because it will be quite terrible travelling that weekend? Perhaps you would let me know. I shall quite understand of course if this is not suitable.
I really am looking forward to having them at home at last and shall be doing everything in my power to ensure they have a good settled home life.
I look forward to having a chat with you when I come for the girls.
Trusting you are well, I look forward to hearing from you.
Yours very sincerely
Phyllis N Norris

Mrs Horne received a letter from Mr Turnbull, the County Children's Officer on 13 June 1966.

Dear Mrs Horne,
Re - Mrs Phyllis Norris of 25 Ambleside Ave Redcar
I thank you for your letter of the 8th June, and I am arranging for Mrs Norris to be visited by a Child Care Officer, in order to obtain an up to date review of the situation in this home, prior to the children returning. When the children do return I will arrange a period of voluntary supervision if Mrs Norris will accept this.
In any event I will do what I can to keep an eye upon these children following their return home, and I shall be writing to you again in due course when I have received the initial report from the Child Care Officer.
Yours sincerely
Mr Turnbull

Mr Morgan, the headmaster of St John's School, sent a letter along with a couple of other necessary documents to Muller's on 17 June, 1966.

Dear Mrs Horne,
Re – Linda Warrior (26-2-55)
I enclose herewith a report on Linda as requested, also her Record Card and a letter about her hearing difficulty. Her Medical Record Card can be obtained from the Central Health Clinic.

Yours faithfully
L. V. W. Morgan
Headmaster

On 18 June, 1966, Muller's wrote to the Education Officer, County Hall, Northallerton.

Dear Sir,
Re – Christine Warrior (27-7-52)
Re – Linda Warrior (26-2-55)
These girls, who have been in the care of these homes since 1957, will be returning to the care of their mother Mrs P N Norris, 25 Ambleside Avenue, Redcar after the end of this school term. Mrs Norris has been to your office in Redcar to consult about appropriate schools and was advised to ask for reports to be sent direct to you. These I now enclose. Christine is in the Grammar stream of a comprehensive school; Linda would have been transferred next term to a secondary school. I hope this gives you the information you require.
Yours faithfully
Mrs Horne

Mrs Horne wrote to my mother on 18 June, 1966.

Dear Mrs Norris,
I have at last got the reports for both girls and sent them today to the Education Department at Northallerton. If you hear nothing in a week or so you had better enquire as their admission to school will need to be arranged before the end of this term. The first weekend in August will not be the Bank Holiday which is now the last Monday or Tuesday.
I do hope things are going on alright? As promised I have written to the local children's officer and had a very friendly reply saying they will get to know you and be prepared to offer any support or help you may need.
With all good wishes,
Yours sincerely
Mrs Horne

Mr. Pragnell, the Child Care Officer, made a visit to my mother at her home in Redcar, after which a letter was sent to Mrs Horne with a report on what he thought about mothers home and if it was suitable to bring Christine and me to live in.

Mr Pragnell wrote to Mrs Horne explaining his visit to mother and Nana's home.

Dear Mrs Horne.
I was fortunate when I visited in finding both Mrs Norris and her mother at home and they were both very friendly and co-operative. Mrs Norris was absent from her employment at the G.E.C factory as she has a slight cold, but hoped to return to work the next day. The home is a three bed-roomed house owned by Redcar Corporation and Mrs Smith holds the tenancy. It is adequately furnished and is clean, tidy and comfortable.
Mrs Norris and her mother eagerly await the return of her girls and Mrs Norris has made enquiries about schools for them. The Redcar Authority is not able to state which schools the girls will attend until their grading are received from the Bristol Authority. Mrs Norris hopes to obtain her divorce in the near future and then intends to make an application to Redcar Housing for a home of her own. She intends to continue with her employment for some time, and Mrs Smith says she will help with the care of the girls whenever required.
My visit disclosed no circumstance which would be against the children returning home, and Mrs Norris stated she will happily accept occasional visits to her home.
I do not consider that regular voluntary supervision is necessary.
C. Pragnell
Child Care Officer

On 23 June, 1966, Mr Turnbull, the County Children's Officer, wrote to Muller's.

Dear Mrs Horne,
Re: Mrs Phyllis Norris
25 Ambleside Avenue Redcar.

*Further to my letter of the 13ᵗʰ June, I have now received the initial
report from Mr Pragnell, Child Care Officer, following his visit to
Mrs Norris, and a copy is enclosed for your information.
You will see that Mr Pragnell's report is quite favourable and I
presume that you will now go ahead with your arrangements for
the return of the children to their mother. In due course, if you will
advise me when the children return, and I will arrange a visit so
that Mr Pragnell can see the children and I will let you have
another report.
Yours sincerely
J. K Turnbull
County Children's Officer*

On 24 June, 1966, Mrs Horne wrote to the County Children's
Officer.

*Dear Mr Turnbull,
Re-Mrs Norris
25 Ambleside Avenue, Redcar
Thank you very much for your prompt help and for Mr. Pragnell re-
assuring report. We expect the two children to return home at the
end of July and I will notify you when they go. We shall be very
glad to know that there is skilful help at hand if needed while they
learn to settle down together.
Yours sincerely
Mrs Horne – Muller's*

It was finally arranged for my mother to travel to
Severnleigh to collect myself and Christine on 30 July, 1966. All
those years living at Muller's and now the time had arrived for us
to leave! There was an air of sadness about leaving but that was
overridden by the excitement of our new life that lay ahead. We
were overjoyed as we had waited so long for this day to arrive. I
was now eleven years old and Christine had just had her
fourteenth birthday a few days before. I was going to live in a
family home with my sister, my mother and my nana. It would be
different this time, not like before when we were little girls and my
mother struggling all the time to make ends meet. Christine and I

would be able to visit friends and they would be able to visit us. We would be allowed to go swimming, roller-skating and do all the things that other kids did as a part of an ordinary family. I was bursting with excitement. We were going to be free!

I just hoped she would turn up to collect us as promised.

I was about to learn what freedom was.

Chapter 19

A NEW LIFE

Another Uncle, Uncle Dennis, a friend of mother's, had kindly offered to take her to Bristol to collect us in his car and drive us all back home to Redcar. He had visited us on occasions with my mother. Just another uncle we thought. Neither of us was aware at that time, but, Uncle Dennis was later to become our stepfather. On Saturday, July 30, 1966 we were woken up a bit later than usual, as it was a Saturday. I was already wide awake and buzzing with excitement. I couldn't get out of my bed quick enough. I dragged the sheets and covers off my bed and threw them onto the floor ready for the laundry, then turned the mattress over and for the first time since being little, I didn't have to remake it. Christine was excitedly flying around upstairs packing her suitcase with the help of the older girls. My suitcase was under my bed and I kept pulling it out to check I had all my belongings. I didn't have a lot of clothes and I would be getting some nice new ones when I got to my new home. Any toys and games I couldn't take, I either gave to one of the other kids or left for everyone to use. Once I'd finished brushing my teeth, I packed my toothbrush and Gibbs toothpaste in the case and closed it. There - that was everything that would fit in. One of the aunties carried my case down the huge staircase for me while I carried my oversized teddy bear.

This magnificent old house, that had been my home for the past nine years and eight months of my life, was now bustling with the excitement of us leaving. The other kids were helping with anything they could and fussing around us. We completed our kitchen chores for the last time on that Saturday morning. I made the toast for one last time, without burning it! We helped peel the spuds and Christine filled the coal scuttles as usual. What a long morning it was becoming, with us anxiously waiting for our mother to arrive. There was the nagging worry she might not turn up, going by past visits. That surely wasn't going to happen today though. Eventually lunchtime came and shortly after mother arrived with her friend, Uncle Dennis. Everyone: Auntie Hilda, all the other auntie's, the children, and even Shawn, whom I was going to miss so dreadfully, were in the hall waiting to see us off and wave goodbye. Jonty had come up with his mum and dad to say his farewells too. It took around an hour before we finally left the house and stepped out onto the driveway to freedom. Uncle Dennis had helped load the car up with our suitcases and few belongings we had accumulated over the last nine, nearly ten years. In a way, it was a sad day as we knew we were going to be missed by the other children and the aunties, but for Christine and me it was the happiest day of our lives.

Everyone was out in the driveway waving us goodbye, I gave Shawn a massive hug, which he kindly returned by standing on his hind legs with his paws on my shoulders licking me to bits with his slavering chops nearly knocking me over.

Uncle Dennis started up the car and we set off on the long journey home to Redcar

While heading north on the motorway we passed by so many people in their cars, all heading towards London with their England flags to watch the football World Cup final. Although it was amusing to see all those cars draped with the England flags, I wasn't bothered. All I wanted to see were the flames rising from the cooling towers at Dorman Long and ICI that had fascinated me so much on my previous visits to Redcar. I yearned to go to the seaside and play on the swings, trampolines and roundabouts, ride on the donkeys and the miniature train on Redcar beach. I wanted to clamber over the rocks where I had gone crab-hunting and more often than not came home soaking wet! I wanted to go to the local swimming baths; the outdoor roller-skating rink; the amusement park where we had spent so much time the previous year with the scary, mad mouse rollercoaster and the waltzers. I was looking forward so much to seeing all my new friends in Ambleside Avenue and Kendal Grove, knowing I could spend as much time as I wanted with them and never have to leave them again.

At approximately 7 p.m. on that Saturday evening after nine years and eight months of living in an orphanage, Christine and I finally arrived at our new home in Ambleside Avenue, Redcar, Yorkshire, for the beginning of our new life as a family with our mother and Nana.

Chapter 20

FINALLY ...

On 2 August, 1966, Muller's wrote to the County Children's Officer.

Dear Mr Turnbull,
With reference to our correspondence in June of this year about
these children's return to their mother, I write now to let you know
that she fetched them home last weekend, the 30th July 1966,
We are very glad to know that you will be continuing some friendly
supervision, and do hope they will settle down and that Mrs Norris
will continue in steady work. We are a little concerned about her
financial position as she seems to be in debt over her divorce
proceedings.
I wrote to your Education Department last June, giving all the
necessary information so that admissions to suitable schools
might be arranged. I have not had any acknowledgement of this
but had also suggested to Mrs Norris that she should get in touch
with the department herself if she had heard nothing nearer the
end of term.
With many thanks for your co-operation
Yours sincerely
Mrs Horne

On 3 August, 1966, Mrs Horne wrote to mother.

Dear Mrs Norris,
I was so sorry not to see you all on Saturday to say goodbye but
was attending the wedding of one of our old girls.
Enclosed are Christine's and Linda's birth certificates which you
may need to show at their new schools. I hope arrangements for
admission to these have been made alright, though I had no
acknowledgement from the Education Department of my letter to
them last June. Would you please sign the enclosed receipt for
the certificates and return it.
We shall remember you all and think of you settling down
together, and hope very much that things will go happily. You will
I'm sure, have realized that it will mean a sacrifice on your part of
very much that you have enjoyed in the way of being free to go

out as much as you want, but I know you want to give yourself first of all, to making a secure and happy home for your girls, and your reward will be in winning their confidence and letting them feel that they can always depend on you whatever happens.
With love to the girls, and all good wishes,
Yours sincerely
Mrs Horne – Muller's.

On 3 August, 1966, K Turnbull, the County Children's Officer, wrote to Muller's.

Dear Mrs Horne

Re-Christine and Linda Warrior
I thank you for your letter of the 2nd August, and I have today requested the Senior Child Officer concerned to visit Mrs Norris and give what assistance he can, following the return of these children to the care of their mother.
In due course I will let you have another report on the children's progress.
Yours sincerely
Mr J.K Turnbull
County Children's Officer

On 7 September, 1966, my mother wrote to Mrs Horne.

Dear Mrs Horne,
I must apologise for not returning the enclosed receipt sooner, I must admit it completely slipped my attention. I have been so busy getting the girls settled in which was very difficult at first as Christine was very homesick for Bristol but I am pleased to say is now settling down nicely. Linda seems to be settled and quite happy. I hope you forgive my erratic writing but I sprained my hand at work and it is rather awkward to write with it at the moment. I will write more at a later date.
So for now God bless you always.
Sincerely yours.
Phyllis N Norris

On 12 September, 1966, Mr. Pragnell the Child Care Officer wrote a report for the attention of Mr Turnbull the County Children's Care Officer on how we were adjusting to our new life and environment.

Dear Mr Turnbull,
I visited this home on the 6th September 1966
Christine and Linda were both at home and had just finished dinner. They have found difficulty in adjusting to their new environment but are gradually integrating themselves with their surroundings.
Christine attends the local youth club activities and Linda is a keen swimmer and roller-skater. They have taken tests to ascertain which schools they will attend but as yet the results have not been forthcoming. Mrs Norris was also at home as she had injured her hand at work.
She informed me that she had obtained her divorce in July but was finding it a struggle financially, as she receives no maintenance from her former husband. He has now four step children to support so it is unlikely that any maintenance can ever be obtained and as Mrs Norris is in full time employment the Ministry of Social Security are unable to assist.
Linda and Christine were both well dressed and seemed to be reasonably happy. They miss their friends in Bristol a great deal, but are fast acquiring new ones in the locality. Linda, very graciously treated me to an impromptu piano solo, whilst Christine was impatiently pressing Linda to accompany her by roller skating. It will obviously take Linda and Christine some time to settle in their new home and to accept their situation, and there will be many crises to be met, but I am sure they can re-adjust and be happy in their life.
I shall visit occasionally to ascertain their progress and Mrs Norris will contact me if my advice and assistance is required.
Mr Pragnell Child Care Officer

Eight months later, Mr Pragnell came to see how we were all getting on and wrote a report which was forwarded to Mrs Horne at Muller's.
I visited these girls on the 5th April 1967. Mrs Norris has now re-married and is living at 8 Far Meadows Lane, Irby, in the Wirral

Cheshire. She is now married to Mr Sowden, who was an old friend of her shipboard days. Mr Sowden is a Chief Officer on large passenger ships.
The girls, Linda and Christine, are both with their mother but Linda is presently staying with her grandmother at Redcar for her Easter holidays. Linda appears to be in good health and is obviously enjoying her holiday very much. She says that she does not like Cheshire very much; she says she much prefers Redcar.
This referral should now be closed as far as this authority is concerned, as these children are not now residing in this area.
Mr Pragnell
Child Care Officer.

On 24 April, 1967, Muller's wrote to Mr Turnbull, Children's Officer.

Dear Mr Turnbull,

Re - Linda and Christine WARRIOR
Thank you for your report on these two girls whose mother is now married and settled outside your area. We are most grateful for your help and kindly interest in them.
Yours Sincerely
Mrs Horne
George Muller Homes for Children

Auntie Hilda invited Christine and me back the following year for a holiday in the summer of 1967. For some strange reason, we were both happy to go back and visit so it can't have been that bad! That was the last time we were there .Auntie Hilda visited Christine and me at my home in Redcar in the summer of 1987. Sadly, she passed away October 1998.

Me, Auntie Hilda and Christine in 1987

My Muller family at Severnleigh

Mr Stan Davey, myself and Mrs Cowan at Alma Road Church in July 2002

ACKNOWLEDGEMENT

Thank you to my big sister, Christine, for all the laughs tears and giggles we had exchanging our memories and piecing them together. It was fun and I'm sure there are a million more we could add. Through our journey together we developed a special bond that will be with us both always.

I'd like to thank Auntie June and Uncle John Hall who still live in Bristol, for the special memories that they shared with me and also for taking the time to help me find George Muller's grave. How amazing it was to stumble across it that day in 2010.

A huge thank you goes out to Wendy, Julian and all the staff at Muller's Administration Office, Cotham Park, Bristol, for being so kind and helpful in July 2002 when I went there to collect my records.

A mention has to go to the now late, Mr Stan Davey, an old Muller boy, who I met during doing my research. He kindly invited both me and my son Robert to join him and the now late, Mrs Cowan, at Alma Road Church for the morning service and then afterwards on to his home for Sunday dinner. I will always appreciate him taking the time to share so many of his memories with me from his days growing up in the Muller Homes.

And finally, love to my mother. I thank her for writing down her memories, without which I couldn't have put this book together. Unfortunately, I didn't finish it in time for her to read the whole story before she passed away on August 19 2013. Thankfully she gave me her blessing and told me to get it finished after she had had the opportunity to read most of it.

Writing this book has been therapeutic and helped me to over-come some of the hurt and bad feelings I have encountered over the years, due to not understanding why I was put into the home. It has taken a long time for me, but I now understand the difficulties she faced and the reasons why she had to make that heart-breaking decision to place myself and my sister Christine in the orphanage.

And so, as this chapter of my life in the George Muller Orphanage ends, the next one begins …

ORPHANED WARRIOR

CONTRIBUTIONS

Literary Editor – Gerry N Mckeown

Editor – Alison Jack

Memories – June and John Hall – Bristol

Memories – Christine Nicholson – (Warrior)

Photographs – Courtesy of Janet and Derek Fisher author of Bygone Bristol Books

Photographs Christine Nicholson - (Warrior)

Photographs – Linda Forrest – (Warrior)

Photographs – Noreen Sowden – (My Mother)

MY INSPIRATION

Books - Michael John Kelly - Just a Boy from Bristol

Books - Christina Noble - Bridge across My Sorrows

Books – Christina Noble - Mama Tina

Books – George Muller Books

📖📖📖

Printed in Great Britain
by Amazon